Communion with God

BOOKS BY NEALE DONALD WALSCH

Conversations with God, book 1

Conversations with God, book 2

Conversations with God, book 3

Conversations with God, book 1 Guidebook

Meditations from Conversations with God, book 1

Meditations from Conversations with God, book 2:
A Personal Journal

The Little Soul and the Sun

Questions and Answers on Conversations with God

Neale Donald Walsch on Relationships

Neale Donald Walsch on Abundance and Right Livelihood

Neale Donald Walsch on Holistic Living

Friendship with God, an Uncommon Dialogue

The Wedding Vows from Conversations with God,
with Nancy Fleming-Walsch

Communion with God

Neale Donald Walsch

G. P. PUTNAM'S SONS

NEW YORK

G.P. Putnam's Sons
Publishers Since 1838
a member of
Penguin Putnam Inc.
375 Hudson Street
New York, NY 10014

Library of Congress Cataloging-in-Publication Data

Walsch, Neale Donald.
Communion with God / Neale Donald Walsch.
p.   cm.
ISBN 0-399-14670-9
1. God—Miscellanea.   2. Spiritual life—Miscellanea.   I. Title.
BF1999.W2278   2000b   00-044560
291.4'4—dc21

Printed in the United States of America

1   3   5   7   9   10   8   6   4   2

This book is printed on acid-free paper. ∞

To God,
with love

Contents

Communion with God

Introduction

Welcome to this book.

I would like you to consider something extraordinary.

I would like you to consider the possibility that this book was created just for you.

If you can accept that construction, I believe you are about to have one of the most powerful experiences of your life.

Now I would like you to consider something even more extraordinary.

I would like you to consider the possibility that this book was created for you *by you.*

If you can imagine a world in which nothing is happening *to* you, and everything is happening *through* you, you will have gotten the message that you intended to send to yourself here within seven sentences.

You can't ask a book to deliver faster than that.

.   .   .

Welcome to this moment.

You are "well come" here, for this moment was designed by you to bring you to the blessed experience you are about to have.

You have sought the answers to life's most meaningful questions, and you have sought them repeatedly, earnestly, and sincerely, or you would not be here.

This search has been going on inside of you, whether you have made it a major part of your exterior life or not; it is what has caused you to pick up this book.

With your understanding of that, you have unraveled one of life's biggest mysteries: *why things happen the way they do.*

All of this in fourteen sentences.

Welcome to this meeting with the Creator.

It is a meeting which you could not have avoided. All people meet with the Creator. It is not a question of whether but of when.

People of earnestness, seeking truth, experience the meeting sooner rather than later. Honesty is a magnet. It attracts Life. And Life is just another word for God.

The person who honestly seeks, honestly receives. Life will not lie to itself.

That is how it has come to pass that you have arrived here, in front of these words. You have placed yourself here, and it has not been by accident. Carefully consider how you got here and you will see that.

Do you believe in the process of Divine Inspiration? I do. I believe in it for you, and I believe in it for me.

Some people don't like it when another says that they've been inspired by God. As I see it, there are several reasons for this.

First, most people don't think _they_ have ever been inspired by God, at least not in the most immediate way—that is, through direct communication—and therefore anyone who makes such a claim is immediately suspect.

Second, claiming that God is one's inspiration appears to be a bit arrogant, implying that the inspiration may not be argued with, nor found lacking in any way, given its origin.

Third, many of those who have claimed Divine Inspiration have not been the easiest people to live with—witness Mozart, Rembrandt, Michelangelo, or any one of a number of popes, as well as countless others who have done some pretty crazy things in the name of God.

Finally, we have made those whom we _do_ believe have been directly inspired by God into such holy men and women that we don't quite know how to deal with them, or how to interact with them in a normal way. Simply put, as wonderful as they are, they can make us uncomfortable.

So we're pretty skittish about this God-is-my-source thing. And, perhaps rightly, we should be. We don't want to swallow whole everything that others tell us, simply because they claim to carry a message from the Most High.

But how can we know for sure what is Divine Inspiration and what is not? How can we be certain who is speaking eternal truth?

Ah, that is the great question. But here is the great secret. We do not have to know. All we have to know is _our_ truth, not someone else's. When we understand this, we understand everything. We understand that what others are saying doesn't have to be The

Truth; it only has to lead us to our own. And it will do that. It cannot help but do that, eventually. All things lead us to *our* innermost truth. *That is their purpose.*

Indeed, that is the purpose of Life itself.

Life is truth, revealing Itself to Itself.

God is Life, revealing Itself to Itself.

You could not stop this process if you wanted to. But you can speed it up.

That is what you are doing here.

That is why you have brought yourself to this book.

This book does not claim to be The Truth. It is intended to guide you to your own innermost wisdom. It is not necessary for you to agree with its contents for it to do that. In fact, agreeing or not agreeing will be irrelevant. If you agree, it will be because you see in this book your own wisdom. If you disagree, it will be because you do not see your own wisdom. In either case, you will have been led back to your own wisdom.

So thank yourself for this book, because it has already brought you back to clarity about one major point: *The highest authority lies within you.*

This is so because each of us has a direct connection to the Divine.

Each of us has the ability to access eternal wisdom. Indeed, I believe that God is inspiring all of us, all of the time. And while all of us have had this experience, some of us have chosen to call it something else:

Serendipity.

Coincidence.

Luck.

Accident.

Freak experience.

Chance encounter.

Perhaps even Divine Intervention.

We seem to be willing to acknowledge that God intervenes in our lives but unable to embrace the idea that God may actually directly inspire us to think, to write, to say, or to do a particular thing. That seems to be going too far.

I'm going to go too far.

I'm going to say that I believe God has inspired me to write this book and you to pick it up. Now let's test this idea against some of the reasons you might have to be skittish about that.

First, I am clear, as I have just said above, that all of us are being inspired by God all of the time. It is not my thought that you and I are unique, or that God has bestowed upon us a singular power, or granted us some special dispensation allowing us to commune with the Divine. I believe that everyone is in a state of such continual communion, and that we may consciously experience this whenever we choose. Indeed, as I understand it, this is the promise of many of the world's religions.

Second, I do not believe that because one is experiencing a moment of open contact with the Divine that one's utterances, actions, or writings are rendered infallible. With all due respect to any religion or movement that claims its founder or its present leader to be infallible, I believe that it *is* possible for divinely inspired people to make errors. And I believe, in fact, that they make them routinely. I do not, therefore, believe that every word of the Bible or the Bhagavad Gita or the Qur'an is literally true, that every utterance of the pope when speaking _ex cathedra_ is correct, or that every action ever taken by Mother Teresa was the right and perfect action for that moment in time. I do believe that Mother Teresa was divinely inspired, but being divinely inspired and being infallible are two different things.

Third, I can be very difficult to live with (nobody knows this more than those who have lived with me), and while I do not claim imperfections for you, I do not think that my own imperfections disqualify me from receiving God's help and direct guidance. In fact, _I believe the opposite is true._

Finally, I don't believe that I am in any danger of becoming "holy" to the point of making anyone uncomfortable. Actually, again, the opposite may be true. If people are uncomfortable with me at all, it is probably because I am not holy enough. It is a challenge to walk my talk. I can write very inspiring things, I can say very inspiring things, but I sometimes catch myself doing things that aren't very inspiring.

I am on a path, and I have by no means reached my destination. Nor, would it appear, am I even getting close. All that is really different between the me of now and the me of yesteryear is that now I have at least _found_ the path. Yet for me that is a great advance. I've spent most of my life not even knowing where I was going, then wondering why I wasn't getting there.

Now I know where I am going. I am going Home, back to the full awareness and experience of my communion with God. And nothing can stop me from getting there. God has promised. And I believe this promise, at last.

God has also shown me the way. Actually, not _the_ way, but _a_ way. For God's greatest truth is that there is not one way only but many ways Home. There are a thousand paths to God, and every one will get you there.

Indeed, all paths lead to God. This is because there is no other place to go.

This book talks about that. It talks about how to go Home. It discusses the experience of Oneness with the Divine, or what I call communion with God. It describes a path to that experience, a pathway through our illusions, to the Ultimate Reality.

This book speaks with one voice. I believe it to be the voice of God, the inspiration of God, the presence of God, moving through me, and through you. If I did not believe that God's voice, God's inspiration, and God's presence could move through all of us, I would have to give up my faith that God could inspire all of the world's religions.

I am not willing to do that. I believe that on this score, religions have it right: God does come into our lives, in real and present ways, and we don't have to be saints or sages for it to happen.

I do not need you to join me in this belief, nor to believe any of the words on these pages. Indeed, I would be happiest if you did not. Do not believe anything you find here.

Know.

Simply know.

Know if any of this is your truth. If it is, it will ring true—for you will have been reunited with your innermost wisdom. If it is not, you will know that, too—once again from having been reunited with your innermost wisdom. In either event, you will have benefited enormously, for you will have experienced, in that moment of reunification, *your own communion with God.*

And that was what you intended when you came here.
To these pages.
And to this planet.

Blesséd be.
Neale Donald Walsch
Ashland, Oregon
July 2000

Prelude

God has spoken to you many times in many ways over many years, but seldom as directly as this.

This time I speak to you *as* You, and that has occurred on only a handful of occasions in the whole of your history.

Few humans have had the courage to hear Me in this way—as themselves. And fewer still have shared with others what they have heard. Those few who have listened, and shared, have changed the world.

Aesop, Confucius, Lao-tzu, Buddha, Muhammad, Moses, and Jesus were among them.

So, too, Chuang Tzu, Aristotle, Huang-po, Sahara, Mahavira, Krishnamurti.

Also, Paramahansa Yogananda, Ramana Maharshi, Kabir, Ralph Waldo Emerson, Thich Nhat Hanh, the Dalai Lama, Elizabeth Clinton.

As well, Sri Aurobindo, Mother Teresa, Meher Baba, Mahatma Gandhi, Kahlil Gibran, Bahá' Alláh, Ernest Holmes, Sai Baba.

Including Joan of Arc, Francis of Assisi, Joseph Smith . . . and more, others, not mentioned here. This list could go on. Yet, relative to the total number of humans who have inhabited your planet, the number is minuscule.

These few have been My messengers—for all have brought forward The Truth within their hearts, as best as they understood it, as purely as they knew how. And while they have each done so through imperfect filters, they have nonetheless brought to your awareness extraordinary wisdom, from which the whole human race has benefited.

What is amazing is how similar their insights have been. Offered at vastly different times and places, separated by legions and centuries, they might just as well have been speaking all at the same time, so tiny have been the variances between them, and so huge the commonalities.

Now it is time to expand this list to include others, living today, as My latest messengers.

We will speak with one voice.

Unless we do not.

You will make that choice, even as you have always done. For in each Moment of Now have you made your decision, and announced it in action.

At the beginning, your thoughts are Mine, and Mine are yours. For at the beginning, it can be no other way. There is only one Source of That Which Is, and the one Source *is* That Which Is.

All things emanate from that Source, then permeate the Is-ness all over, and reveal themselves as Individuations of the Whole.

The individual interpretations of the one message produce the miracle of Oneness in many forms.

This Oneness in many forms is what you call Life.

Life is God, interpreted. That is, *translated* into many forms.

The first level of translation is from the unified non-physical to the individuated non-physical.

The second level of translation is from the individuated non-physical to the individuated physical.

The third level of translation is from the individuated physical into the unified physical.

The fourth level of translation is from the unified physical into the unified non-physical.

Then the cycle of Life is complete.

The continuing process of the translation of God produces endless variety within God's unity. This variety of the unity is what I have called "individuation." It is the individual expression of that which is not separate but which can be individually expressed.

The purpose of individual expression is for Me to experience My Self as the whole, through the experiencing of My parts. And while the whole is greater than the sum of the parts, I can only experience this by knowing the sum.

And that is who you are.

You are the Sum of God.

I have told you this many times before, and many of you have heard this as the *son* of God. That, too, is correct. You are the sons, and daughters, of God. Yet it does not matter what labels or names you use, it adds up to the same thing: You are The Sum of God.

So, too, is everything around you. Everything that you see, and do not see. All That Is, All That Ever Was, and All That Ever Will Be is Me. And all that I am, I am now.

I Am That I Am—as I have told you many times.

There is nothing that I have ever been that I have ceased to be. And there is nothing that I will ever be that I am not now. I cannot become anything that I now am not, nor can I fail to be anything that I once was.

This is as it was in the beginning, is now, and ever shall be, world without end. Amen.

I am coming to you now, in this day and time, as you begin another millennium, so that you may start a new thousand years in a new way: knowing Me at last, choosing Me first, and being Me always, all ways.

There is no mistake in the timing. I began these new revelations early in the last decade, continued My conversations with you throughout the last years of the century, and in the final moments of the last millennium reminded you how you may have a friendship with Me.

Now, in the first year of the new millennium, I speak to you with one voice, that we may experience communion.

Should you choose this experience of communion with God, you will finally know peace, and joy unbounded, and love fully expressed, and full freedom.

Should you choose this truth, you will change your world.

Should you choose this reality, you will create it, and at last fully experience Who You Really Are.

It will be the hardest thing you have ever done, and the easiest thing you will ever do.

It will be the hardest thing you have ever done because you will have to deny who you think you are, and stop denying Me. It will be the easiest thing you will ever do because there will be nothing that you have to do.

All you have to do is be, and all you have to be is Me.

Even this will not be an act of will but a simple acknowledgment. It will not require an action, only an admission.

I have been seeking this admission forever. When you grant Me admission, you let Me into your life. You admit that you and I are One. This is your ticket to heaven. It says: *Admit One.*

When I gain entrance into your heart, you gain entrance into heaven. And your heaven can be on Earth. Everything can truly be "on earth as it is in heaven" when the time of separation is over and the time of unification is at hand.

Unification with Me, and unification with all others, and with every living thing.

This is what I have come to tell you, once more, through the messengers of today. You will know them as My messengers because they will all be bringing the same message:

We Are All One.

This is the only message that matters. It is the only message there is. Everything else in Life is a reflection of this message. Everything else sends it.

The fact that you have so far failed to receive it (you have *heard* it often, but you have failed to *receive it*) is what has caused every misery, every sorrow, every conflict, every heartache in your experience. It has caused every murder, every war, every rape and robbery, every assault and attack, mental, verbal, and physical. It has caused every illness and dis-ease, and every encounter with what you call "death."

The idea that we are *not* One is an illusion.

Most people believe in God: They just don't believe in a God who believes *in them.*

God does believe in them. And God loves them more than most of them know.

The idea that God turned stone-silent and stopped talking to the human race a long time ago is false.

The idea that God is angry with the human race and kicked it out of Paradise is false.

The idea that God has set Himself up as judge and jury and will be deciding whether members of the human race go to heaven or hell is false.

God loves every human being who ever lived, lives now, or ever will live.

God's desire is for every soul to return to God, and God cannot fail in having this desire fulfilled.

God is separate from nothing, and nothing is separate from God.

There is nothing that God needs, because God is everything there is.

This is the good news. Everything else is an illusion.

The human race has been living with illusions for a long

time. This is not because the human race is stupid, but because the human race is very smart. Humans have understood intuitively that illusions have a purpose, and a very important one. Most humans have simply forgotten that they know this.

And they have forgotten that _their forgetting is itself part of what they have forgotten_—and therefore part of the illusion.

Now it is time for humans to remember.

You are one of those who will lead the vanguard in this process. There is nothing surprising in this, given what has been going on in your life.

You have come to this book to remember The Illusions Of Humans, so that you may never again be caught up in them but achieve communion with God once more in the living of your life through the awareness of Ultimate Reality.

It is perfect that you have done so. And it is, obviously, not happenstance.

You have come here so that you may know _experientially_ that God resides within you, that you may have, whenever you wish, a meeting with the Creator.

The Creator may be experienced and found within you and all around you. But you must look past The Illusions Of Humans. You must ignore them.

Here are The Ten Illusions. Get to know them well so that you will recognize them when you encounter them.

1. Need Exists
2. Failure Exists
3. Disunity Exists

4. Insufficiency Exists

5. Requirement Exists

6. Judgment Exists

7. Condemnation Exists

8. Conditionality Exists

9. Superiority Exists

10. Ignorance Exists

The first five of these are the Physical Illusions, having to do with life in your physical body. The second five are the Metaphysical Illusions, having to do with non-physical realities.

In this communication, each of these illusions will be explored in detail. You will see how each has been created, and you will see how each has affected your life. And before this communication is complete, you will also see how you can undo any effects of these illusions that you wish to undo.

Now, the first step in the process of any really open communication is that you must be willing to suspend your disbelief about what you are hearing. You will be asked to do that here. Please temporarily give up any previous notions you may have about God and Life. You may return to your previous ideas at any time. It is not a question of abandoning them forever but of merely setting them aside for the moment to *allow for the possibility that there may be something you do not know, the knowing of which could change everything.*

Examine, for instance, your reaction to the idea that God is communicating with you right now.

In your past, you have found all sorts of reasons not to accept that you could have an actual conversation with God.

I'm going to ask you to set those thoughts aside and assume that you are receiving this communication directly from Me.

To make it easier on you, I will speak of Myself in the third person through much of this communication. I recognize that it may be a little unnerving for you to hear Me using the first person singular. And so, while I will do it once in a while (just to remind you who is bringing you this information), I will most of the time speak of Myself as, simply, God.

While your receiving a direct communication from the Deity may seem improbable to you at first, understand that you have come to this communication to remember, at last, Who You Really Are, and the illusions that you have created. Soon, you will deeply understand that you have actually caused this book to come to you. For now, simply hear Me when I tell you that in most of the moments of your life, *you are living an illusion.*

The Ten Illusions Of Humans are very big, very powerful illusions that you created during the earliest part of your experience on Earth. And you create hundreds of smaller ones every day. Because you believe them, you have created a cultural story that allows you to live these Illusions and thus make them real.

They are not *really real,* of course. Yet you have created an Alice in Wonderland world in which they seem very real, indeed. And like the Mad Hatter, you will deny that what is False is false, and that what is Real is real.

You have, in fact, been doing this for a very long time.

A cultural story is a story that has been handed down from generation to generation, across centuries and millennia. It is the story that you tell yourself about yourself.

Because your cultural Story is based on illusions, it produces myths rather than an understanding of reality.

The cultural story of Humans is that

1. God has an agenda. (Need Exists)
2. The outcome of life is in doubt. (Failure Exists)
3. You are separate from God. (Disunity Exists)
4. There is not enough. (Insufficiency Exists)
5. There is something you have to do. (Requirement Exists)
6. If you do not do it, you will be punished. (Judgment Exists)
7. The punishment is everlasting damnation. (Condemnation Exists.)
8. Love is, therefore, conditional. (Conditionally Exists)
9. Knowing and meeting the conditions renders you superior. (Superiority Exists)
10. You do not know that these are illusions. (Ignorance Exists)

This cultural story has been so ingrained in you that you now live it fully and completely. This, you tell each other, "is just the way it is."

You have been telling each other that now for many centuries. Indeed, for millennia after millennia. For so long, in fact, that myths have grown up around these illusions and stories. Some of the most prominent myths have been reduced to concepts, such as . . .

- Thy will be done.
- Survival of the fittest.
- To the victor go the spoils.
- You were born in Original Sin.
- The wages of sin are death.
- Vengeance is Mine, sayeth the Lord.
- What you don't know won't hurt you.
- God only knows.

. . . and many others, equally destructive and non-serving.

Based on these illusions, stories, and myths—none of which has anything to do with Ultimate Reality—here is how many humans have come to think about Life:

"We are born into a hostile world, run by a God who has things He wants us to do and things He wants us not to do, and will punish us with everlasting torture if we don't get the two right.

"Our first experience in Life is separation from our mother, the Source of our Life. This creates the context for our entire reality, which we experience as one of separation from the Source Of All Life.

"We are not only separate from all Life but from everything else in Life. Everything that exists, exists separate from us. And we are separate from everything else that exists. We do not want it this way, but this is the way it is. We wish it were otherwise, and, indeed, we strive for it to be otherwise.

"We seek to experience Oneness again with all things, and especially with each other. We may not know why, exactly, yet it seems almost instinctual. It feels like the natural thing to do. The only problem is, there does not seem to be enough of the other to satisfy us. No mat-

ter what the other thing is that we want, we cannot seem to get enough of it. We cannot get enough love, we cannot get enough time, we cannot get enough money. We cannot get enough of whatever it is we think we need in order to be happy and fulfilled. The moment we think that we have enough, we decide that we want more.

"Since there is 'not enough' of whatever it is we think we need to be happy, we must 'do stuff' to get as much as we can get. Things are required of us in exchange for everything, from God's love to the natural bounty of Life. Simply 'being alive' is not enough. Therefore we, like all of Life, are not enough.

"Because just 'being' isn't sufficient, the competition begins. If there's not enough out there, we have to compete for what's there.

"We have to compete for everything, including God.

"This competition is tough. It is about our very survival. In this contest, only the fittest survive. And to the victor go all the spoils. If we lose, we live a hell on Earth. And after we die, if we are losers in the competition for God, we experience hell again—this time forever.

"Death was actually created by God because our forebears made the wrong choices. Adam and Eve had everlasting life in the Garden of Eden. But then, Eve ate the fruit of the tree of the Knowledge of Good and Evil, and she and Adam were driven from the Garden by an angry God. This God sentenced them, and all their progeny forevermore, to death as the first punishment. Henceforth, life in the body would be limited, and no longer everlasting, and so would the stuff of Life.

"Yet God will give us back our everlasting life if we never again break His rules. God's love is unconditional, it is only God's rewards which are not. God loves us even as He condemns us to everlasting damnation. It hurts Him more than it hurts us, because He really _wants us to return home, but He can't do anything about it if we misbehave. The choice is ours._

"The trick is, therefore, to not misbehave. We need to live a good life. We must strive to do so. In order to do so, we have to know the truth about what God wants and does not want from us. We cannot please God, and we cannot avoid offending Him, if we do not know right from wrong. So we have to know the truth about that.

"The truth is simple to understand and easy to know. All we have to do is listen to the prophets, teachers, sages, and the source and founder of our religion. If there is more than one religion and, therefore, more than one source and founder, then we have to make sure to pick the right one. Picking the wrong one could result in us being a loser.

"When we pick the right one, we are superior, we are better than our peers, because we have the truth on our side. This state of being 'better' allows us to claim most of the prizes in the contest without actually contesting them. We get to declare ourselves the winners before the competition begins. _It is out of this awareness that we give ourselves all the advantages, and write our 'Rules of Life' in such a way that certain others find it nearly impossible to win the really big prizes._

"We do not do this out of meanness but simply in order to ensure that victory is ours—as rightly it should be, since it is those of our religion, of our nationality, of our race, of our gender, of our political persuasion who know the truth, and therefore deserve to be winners.

"Because we deserve to win, we have a right to threaten others, to fight with them, even to kill them if necessary, in order to produce this result.

"There may be another way to live, another thing that God has in mind, another, larger truth, but if there is, we don't know it. In fact, *it is not clear whether we are even* supposed *to know it. It is possible that we are not supposed to even try to know it, much less to truly know and understand God. To try is presumptuous, and to declare that you have actually done so is blasphemous.*

"God is the Unknown Knower, the Unmoved Mover, the Great Unseen. Therefore, we cannot know the truth that we are required to know *in order to meet the conditions* that we are required to meet *in order to receive the love* that we are required to receive *in order to avoid the condemnation* that we are seeking to avoid *in order to have the everlasting life* that we had before any of this started.

"Our ignorance is unfortunate, but should not be problematic. All we need do is take what we think we do *know—our cultural story—on faith, and proceed accordingly. This we have tried to do, each according to his or her own beliefs, and thus we have produced the life that we are now living, and the reality on Earth that we are creating."*

This is how most of the human race has it constructed. You each have your minor variations, but this is, in essence, how you live your lives, justify your choices, and rationalize the outcomes.

Some of you do not accept all of this, yet all of you accept some of it. And you accept these statements as the operating reality not because they reflect your innermost wisdom but because *someone else has told you that they are true.*

At some level, you have had to make yourself believe them.

This is called make-believe.

Yet now it is time to move away from make-believe and toward what is real. This will not be easy, because Ultimate Reality will differ a great deal from what many people in your world are now agreeing is real. You will literally have to be "in this world, but not of it."

And what would be the purpose of that if your life is going well? Nothing. There would be no purpose. If you are satisfied with your life and with the world as it is, there would no reason for you to seek to shift your reality and to stop all this make-believe.

This message is for those who are not satisfied with their world as it is.

We shall now examine The Ten Illusions one by one. You will see how each illusion has caused you to create life on your planet as you are now living it.

You will notice that each illusion builds on the previous. Many sound very much alike. That is because they _are_ alike. All of the illusions are simply variations on The First Illusion. They are grander distortions of the original distortion.

You will also notice that each new illusion was created to fix a flaw in the illusion just before. Finally, tired of fixing flaws, you simply decided that you did not understand any of it. Thus the final Illusion: Ignorance Exists.

This allowed you to shrug your shoulders and quit trying to solve the mystery.

But the evolving mind would not allow such a retreat for very long. In just a few short millennia—a very brief time, indeed, in the history of the Universe—you have come to the place where ignorance is no longer bliss.

You are about to climb out of primitive culture. You are about to make a quantum leap in your understandings. You are about to see through . . . THE TEN ILLUSIONS.

PART I

The Ten Illusions of Humans

1.

The Illusion of Need

The First Illusion is:

NEED EXISTS

This is not only The First Illusion, but the grandest. On this illusion are all other illusions based.

Everything that you currently experience in life, everything that you feel moment to moment, is rooted in this idea, and your thoughts about it.

Need is non-existent in the Universe. One needs something only if one requires a particular result. The Universe does not require a particular result. The Universe *is* the result.

Need is likewise non-existent in the mind of God. God would need something only if God required a particular result. God does not require any particular result. God is that which produces *all* results.

If God needed something to produce a result, where would God get it? There is nothing that exists outside of God.

God is All That Is, All That Was, and All That Will Ever Be. There is nothing that is that is not God.

You may better grasp this idea if you use the word "Life" in place of the word "God." The two words are interchangeable, so you will not alter the meaning; you will merely increase your understanding.

Nothing that is, is not Life. If Life needed something to produce a result, where would Life get it? There is nothing that exists outside of Life. Life is All That Is, All That Was, and All That Will Ever Be.

God needs nothing to occur except that which is occurring.

Life needs nothing to occur except that which is occurring.

The Universe needs nothing to occur except that which is occurring.

This is the nature of things. _This_ is how it is, not the way you have imagined it.

In your imagination you have created the idea of Need out of your experience that you need things in order to survive. Yet suppose that you didn't care whether you lived or died. Then what would you need?

Nothing at all.

And suppose that it was impossible for you _not_ to live. Then what would you need?

Nothing at all.

Now here is the truth about you: It is impossible for you not to survive. You cannot _fail_ to live. It is not a question of _whether_ you will live but _how._ That is, what form will you take? What will your experience be?

I tell you this: You need nothing to survive. Your survival is guaranteed. I gave you everlasting life, and I never took it away from you.

Hearing this, you may say yes, but survival is one thing, and happiness is another. You may imagine that you need something in order to survive *happily*—that you can be happy only under certain conditions. This is not true, but you have believed it to be true. And because belief produces experience, you have experienced life in this way, and have thus imagined a God who must experience Life in this way as well. Yet this is no more true for God than it is for you. The only difference is, God *knows this*.

When *you* know this, you will be as God. You will have mastered life, and your whole reality will change.

Now here is a great secret: Happiness is not created as a result of certain conditions. Certain conditions are created as a result of happiness.

That is such an important statement that it bears repeating.

Happiness is not created as a result of certain conditions. Certain conditions are created as a result of happiness.

This statement holds true for every other state of being as well.

Love is not created as a result of certain conditions. Certain conditions are created as a result of love.

Compassion is not created as a result of certain conditions. Certain conditions are created as a result of compassion.

Abundance is not created as a result of certain conditions. Certain conditions are created as a result of abundance.

Substitute any state of being you can imagine or devise. It

will still hold true that Beingness precedes experience, and produces it.

Because you have not understood this, you have imagined certain things must occur in order for you to be happy—and you also imagine a God for whom the same is true.

Yet if God is First Cause, what can occur that God did not cause in the first place? And if God is all-powerful, what can occur that God does not choose to occur?

Is it possible for something to occur that God cannot stop? And if God is choosing *not* to stop it, is the occurrence itself not something which God is choosing?

Of course it is.

Yet why would God choose things to occur that would make God unhappy? The answer is an answer that you cannot accept.

Nothing makes God unhappy.

You cannot believe this because it would require you to believe in a God without need or judgment, and you cannot imagine such a God. The reason that you cannot imagine such a God is that you cannot imagine such a *human.* You do not believe that *you* can live that way—and *you cannot imagine a God who is greater than you.*

When you come to understand that you *can* live that way, then you will know all there is to know about God.

You will know that your second assessment was right. God is *not* greater than you. How can God be? For God is That Which Is You, and you are That Which Is God. Yet *you* are greater than you think you are.

Masters know this. There are Masters walking your planet

right now who know this. These Masters come from many traditions, religions, and cultures, yet they all have one thing in common.

Nothing makes Masters unhappy.

In the early days of your primitive culture, most humans were not in this place of mastery. Their only desire was to avoid unhappiness, or pain. Their awareness was too limited for them to understand that pain did not have to produce unhappiness, and so their life strategy was built around what later came to be described as The Pleasure Principle. They moved toward what brought them pleasure and moved away from what deprived them of pleasure (or caused pain).

Thus, The First Illusion, the idea that Need Exists, was born. It was what could be called the first mistake.

Need does not exist. It is a fiction. In reality, you need nothing to be happy. Happiness is a state of mind.

This is not something that early humans were capable of grasping. And because they felt that they needed certain things in order to be happy, they assumed that the same must be true of all Life. Included in that assumption was that part of Life which they came to understand as a Greater Power— a power that succeeding generations have conceptualized as a living being referred to by a wide variety of names, among them Allah, Yahweh, Jehovah, and God.

It was not difficult for early humans to conceive of a power greater than themselves. Indeed, it was necessary. An explanation was needed for things that happened that were totally out of their control.

The mistake here was not in assuming that there was such

a thing as God (the combined power and the combined energy of All That Is), but in assuming that this Total Power and Complete Energy could need anything at all; that God was, in some way, dependent on something or someone else to be happy or satisfied, complete or fulfilled.

This was like saying that The Fullness was not full, that it needed something to *make* it full. It was a contradiction in terms—but they could not see this. Many still do not see it today.

From this creation of a dependent God, people produced a cultural story in which God has an *agenda.* In other words, there are things God wants and needs to occur, and *ways* in which they *must* occur, in order for God to be happy.

Humans have reduced this cultural story to a myth that has crystallized as: Thy Will be done.

Your idea that I *had* a Will forced you to then try to figure out what My Will *was.* This exercise quickly made it clear that there was no universal agreement among your species on this point. And if not everyone knew, or agreed on, what God's Will was, not everyone could possibly be *doing* God's Will.

The cleverest among you used this rationale to explain why some people's lives seemed to work better than others. But then you forced a new question: How could it be possible for God's Will not to be done if God was God?

Clearly, there was a flaw in that First Illusion. This should have revealed the idea of Need as false. But humans knew at some very deep level that they could not *give up* the Illusion, or something very vital would come to an end.

They were right. But they made a mistake. Instead of

seeing the Illusion *as* an illusion, and using it for the purpose for which it was intended, they thought they had to *fix its flaw.*

Thus, it was to fix the flaw in The First Illusion that The Second Illusion was created.

2.

The Illusion of

Failure

The Second Illusion is:

FAILURE EXISTS

The idea that God's Will (assuming that God has one) could *not* be done runs counter to everything you thought you knew about God—namely, that God is all-powerful, ever-present, the Supreme Being, the Creator—but it is one that you nevertheless enthusiastically embraced.

This produced the highly improbable but very powerful illusion that *God can fail.* God can desire something but not get it. God can wish for something but not receive it. God can need something but not have it.

In short, God's Will can be thwarted.

This illusion was quite a stretch, for even the limited perceptions of the human mind could spot the contradiction. Yet your species has a rich imagination and can stretch credibility to the limit with amazing ease. You have not only imagined a God with needs, you have imagined a God who can fail to have His needs met.

How have you done this? Once again, through the use of projection. Your have projected yourself upon your God.

Once again, an ability or quality of being which you have ascribed to God has been derived directly from your own experience. Since you noticed that *you* could fail to obtain all the things that you imagine you need to be happy, you have declared that the same is true of God.

From this illusion you have created a cultural story which teaches that the outcome of life is in doubt.

It could work out, or it could not. It might be okay, and it might not. It will all be fine in the end—unless it isn't.

Adding doubt to the mix—doubt that God could meet His needs (assuming I had any)—produced your first encounter with fear.

Prior to contriving this story of a God who could not always get His way, you had no fear. There was nothing *to* fear. God was in charge, God was All Power, All Wonder and Glory, and all was right with the world. What could go wrong?

But then came the idea that God could want something and actually not get it. God could want all of His children to return to Him in heaven, but His children themselves, by their own actions, could prevent this.

Yet this idea, too, strained credibility, and again the human mind saw the contradiction. How could God's creations thwart the Creator if the Creator and the creations were one? How could the outcome of life be in doubt if the One producing the outcome and the One experiencing it were the same?

Clearly, there was a flaw in The Second Illusion. This should have revealed the idea of Failure to be false, but humans knew at some very deep level that they could not *give up* the Illusion, or something very vital would come to an end.

Again, they were right. But again, they made a mistake. Instead of seeing the Illusion *as* an illusion, and using it for the purpose for which it was intended, they thought they had to *fix the flaw.*

It was to fix the flaw in The Second Illusion that The Third Illusion was created.

3.

The Illusion of

Disunity

The Third Illusion is:

DISUNITY EXISTS

The only escape from the conundrum of The Second Illusion was to create a third: The Creator and the creations were *not* all one.

This required the human mind to conceive of the possibility of the impossible—that That Which Is One is not One; that That Which Is Unified is really separate.

This is the Illusion of Disunity—the idea that separation exists.

Your species reasoned that if creations were separate from the Creator, and if the Creator allowed the creations to do whatever they pleased, it would then be possible for the creations to do something *that the Creator did not want them to do.* Under these circumstances, the Will of the Creator could be thwarted. God could want something but not get it.

Disunity produces the possibility of Failure, and Failure is only possible if Need exists. One illusion depends upon another.

The first three illusions are the most crucial. So important are these illusions, so key are they in supporting the rest, that separate cultural stories were assigned to them in order to explain them, and to assure that they _would be_ explained, clearly and often.

Each of your cultures created its own special story, but all of them made the same basic points, each in their own way. One of the most famous is the story of Adam and Eve.

It is said that the first man and the first woman were created by God and lived happily in the Garden of Eden, or Paradise. There they enjoyed eternal life and communion with the Divine.

In exchange for this gift of Life idyllic, God is said to have required only one thing. Do not, He commanded, eat of the fruit of the Tree of the Knowledge of Good and Evil.

According to this legend, Eve ate of the fruit anyway. She disobeyed orders. But it was not entirely her fault. She was tempted by a serpent, who in reality was a being you have called Satan, or the Devil.

And just who is this Devil? He is, one story has it, an angel gone bad, a creation of God who dared to want to be as great as his Creator. This, the story says, is the ultimate offense, the supreme blasphemy. All creations should honor the Creator and never seek to be as great, or greater.

In this particular version of the main cultural story you have deviated from your normal pattern by ascribing to Me certain qualities that are *not* reflected in human experience.

Human creators actually *want* their offspring to strive to be as great, if not greater, than they. It is the greatest pleasure of all healthy parents to see their children reach, and exceed, their own station in life and to surpass their own achievements.

God, on the other hand, was said to have been dishonored by this, and deeply offended. Satan, the fallen angel, was cast away, separated from the flock, shunned, damned, and suddenly there were two powers in Ultimate Reality, God and Satan; and two places from which they operated, heaven and hell.

It was Satan's desire, according to the story that developed, to tempt humans to disobey the Will of God. God and Satan were now in competition for man's soul. And, fascinatingly, this was a competition that *God could lose.*

All of this proved that I was not an all-powerful God after all . . . or that I *was* all-powerful, but didn't want to use My power, because I wanted to give Satan a fair chance. *Or,* that it wasn't about giving Satan a fair chance, it was about giving human beings free will. *Except* that if you *exercised* your free will in a way I did not approve of, I would hand you over to Satan, who would torture you for eternity.

Such are the convoluted stories that have grown into religious doctrine on your planet.

In the story of Adam and Eve, many people believed I punished the first man and the first woman for Eve's eating of the forbidden fruit by casting them out of the Garden of Eden.

And (if you can believe this), *I punished every other man and woman who ever lived after that,* burdening them with the first humans' guilt, and sentencing them to also be separate from Me throughout their lives on earth.

Through this and other equally colorful stories, the first three illusions were conveyed in a dramatic fashion that children, in particular, would not soon forget. So successful were these stories in injecting fear into the hearts of children that they were repeated over and over to each new generation. Thus the first three illusions were deeply imbedded in the human psyche.

1. God has an agenda. (Need Exists)
2. The outcome of life is in doubt. (Failure Exists)
3. You are separate from God. (Disunity Exists)

While the idea that Need and Failure exists is crucial to the rest of the Illusions, the idea that Disunity Exists has the most impact on human affairs.

The impact of The Third Illusion is felt by the human race to this day.

If your thought about The Third Illusion is that it is true, you shall have one experience of life.

If your thought is that it is not true, but is, in fact, an illusion, you shall have another.

These two experiences will be dramatically different.

Currently, nearly everyone on your planet believes The Illusion of Disunity to be real. As a result, people feel separate from God and separate from each other.

The feeling of separation from Me makes it extremely difficult for people to relate to Me in any meaningful way. They either misunderstand Me, or fear Me, or they beg for My help—or they deny Me altogether.

In so doing, humans have missed a glorious opportunity to use the most powerful force in the Universe. They have subjected themselves to lives over which they imagine they have no control, under conditions they think they cannot change, producing experiences and outcomes they believe they cannot escape.

They live lives of quiet desperation, offering up their pain, suffering it gladly, believing that their silent bravery will earn them sufficient favor to get into heaven, where they will receive their reward.

There are many reasons that suffering without undue complaining may be good for the soul, but ensuring one's reward in heaven is not one of them. Courage is its own reward, and there can never be a good reason to cause other people suffering—which is what complaining does.

The Master, therefore, never complains, and so, limits the suffering outside of himself—and inside as well. Yet, the Master does not refrain from complaining *in order* to limit suffering, but because the Master does not interpret the experience of pain as suffering, but simply as pain.

Pain is an experience. Suffering is a judgment which is made about that experience. The judgment of many is that the pain they are experiencing is not okay, and should not be occurring. Yet the degree to which pain is accepted as perfect is the degree to which suffering in life may be eliminated. It is through this understanding that Masters overcome all suffering, although they may not escape all pain.

Even people who have not achieved mastery have experienced the difference between pain and suffering. An example of this might be having a badly aching tooth pulled. It hurts to have the tooth pulled, but it is very welcome pain.

Their feeling of separation from Me prevents humans from using Me, calling upon Me, having a friendship with Me, harnessing the full potential of My creative and healing power, either to end suffering, or for any other purpose.

Their feeling of separation from each other allows humans to do all manner of things to each other that they would never do to themselves. By failing to see that they *are* doing these things to themselves, they produce and reproduce unwelcome results in their daily lives and in their planetary experience.

It has been said that the human race is facing the same problems that it has faced since the dawn of recorded history—and this is true, but to a lesser degree all the time. Greed, violence, jealousy, and other behaviors that you do not believe benefit anyone are still displayed by members of your species, although now by the minority. This is a sign of your evolution.

Yet efforts in your society are directed not nearly so much at seeking to change these behaviors as seeking to punish them. It is thought that punishing them will correct them. Some people are still not understanding that until they correct the conditions in society which *create* and *invite* unwanted behaviors, they will correct nothing.

A truly objective analysis proves this, yet many people ignore that proof and continue trying to solve society's problems with the same energy that created them. They seek to end killing with killing, to end violence with violence, to quell anger with anger. In doing all of this, they fail to see their hypocrisy, and thus embody it.

Recognizing the first three Illusions *as* illusions would stop everyone from denying the Oneness of all Life and threatening to destroy all life on your planet.

Many humans continue to see themselves as separate from each other, from all other living things, and from God. They see that they are destroying themselves, yet they claim not to understand how they are doing it. Surely, they say, it is not through their individual actions. They cannot see the connection between their individual decisions and choices and the world at large.

These are the beliefs of many, and, if you wish to see them changed, it is up to you who truly understand Cause and Effect to change them. For your fellow humans believe that it is having no negative effect on The Whole to cut down hundreds of thousands of trees each week so that they can have their Sunday paper.

It is having no negative effect on The Whole to pump impurities of every sort into the atmosphere so that they can have their lifestyles unchanged.

It is having no negative effect on The Whole to use fossil fuels rather than solar-powered energy.

It is having no negative effect on The Whole to smoke cigarettes, or eat red meat at every meal, or consume large quantities of alcohol, and they're tired of people telling them that it is.

It is having *no negative effect,* they say, and they're tired of people telling them that it is.

Individual human behaviors, they tell themselves, are not having such a negative effect on The Whole that they could actually cause The Whole to *collapse.* That would only be possible if there was nothing that was separate—if, in effect, The Whole was doing all of this to itself. And that is silly. The Third Illusion is true. *We are separate.*

Still, the separate actions of all the separate beings who are not one with each other, and not one with all of Life, seem, in fact, to have a very real effect on Life itself. Now, at last, more and more humans are beginning to acknowledge this as they develop from primitive cultural thinking into a more evolved society.

This is because of the work that you, and others like you, are doing. For you have raised your voice. You have sounded the alarm. You have joined the effort to awaken each other, each in your own way, some quietly and individually, some in groups.

In days gone by, there were not nearly as many of you ready and able to awaken the others. And so the mass of people lived deep within the illusions, and were puzzled. Why should the fact that they are separate from each other create a problem? How is it that anything other than communal living—one for all, and all for one—could not be made to work without struggle?

These are the questions humans began to ask.

Clearly, there was a flaw in The Third Illusion. This should have revealed the idea of Disunity to be false, but humans knew at some very deep level that they could not *give up* the Illusion, or something very vital would come to an end.

Again, they were right. But again, they made a mistake.

Instead of seeing the Illusion *as* an illusion, and using it for the purpose for which it was intended, they thought they had to *fix the flaw.*

It was to fix the flaw in The Third Illusion that The Fourth Illusion was created.

4.

The Illusion of
Insufficiency

This is The Fourth Illusion:

It arises out of The Third Illusion, for without the idea of Disunity, the idea of Insufficiency is insupportable. If there is only One Thing, and that One Thing Is All That Is, there can be no insufficiency of any kind, because that One Thing is everything, and thus . . .

It is sufficient unto Itself.

This is a statement of the nature of God.

This is not, however, the experience of humans, *because humans imagine themselves to be separate from God,* and separate from each other as well. Yet no human is separate from God, since God is Everything that is. Therefore humans are not, and *cannot* be, separate from each other.

This is a statement of the nature of humans.

It would be inaccurate to conclude that the idea of Disunity was a "bad idea," that it did not serve your purpose. Indeed, the idea of separation was a *blessed* idea, allowing The Whole to understand that it was the sum of its parts, and even greater still. The illusion serves your purpose magnificently *when you use the illusion as a tool to create experience.*

When you forget that separation is an illusion, you imagine that it is the real state of things. The illusion no longer creates experience, it *becomes* experience.

It is like feigning anger to make someone else more solicitous, and then actually becoming angry. Or feigning interest in someone in order to make someone else jealous, only to find that the illusion of interest has become very real indeed . . .

The device becomes the experience.

By this process you have come to actually believe that you are separate; that Disunity is possible in the unified field you call the Universe.

Now, I have described The Third Illusion as the most powerful Illusion, and that is true. It has had enormous impact on your day-to-day experience. Most significantly, your belief in separation has led to your idea that there is "not enough."

When there was only One Thing, and you knew that you *were* that One Thing, there was never a question of there not being enough. There was always enough of you. But when you decided that there was *more* than One Thing, then (and only then) could it appear that there was not enough of the other thing.

This "other thing" that you think there is, is the stuff of Life. Yet you *are* Life, and that which Life *is*—which is God, Itself.

Still, as long as you imagine that you are separate from God, you will imagine that you are something other than what God is—which is Life itself. You may think that you are that which *lives,* but you will not imagine yourself to be Life Itself.

This separation *of* Itself *from* Itself is what you have called the casting out from the Garden of Eden. Suddenly, where once there was eternal life, now there is death. Suddenly, where once there was abundance, now there is not enough.

Suddenly, it seems that there are many aspects of life competing for Life Itself. This is impossible in Ultimate Reality, but not in your imagination. You can even imagine that *you* are in competition—with the birds, with the bees, with every other living thing and all other human beings.

You can create a nightmare in which all that supports your life seems to limit it. Thus, you will actually attempt to subdue that which supports you.

You were told to have *dominion,* but you have decided that this means *domination.* So you have actually begun a war with nature, and with the natural order of things.

You have used science and technology to twist and turn and manipulate nature so that it bends to your will. You are slowly destroying nature as it naturally is in an attempt to experience yourself as you already naturally are.

You already are what you seek to be—eternal, unlimited, and one with all—yet you do not remember this. And so, you seek to subdue Life in order that you may have more abundant Life. And you do not even see what you are doing.

Life becomes the single common denominator. Everyone wants Life, and the things that support Life. And, because you think there is more than one of you, you are afraid that there may not be enough Life to go around.

Out of this fear you produce your next imagined reality: death.

A life that you thought to be eternal (until you imagined that you were separate, it never occurred to you that you would not always "be") now seems to have a beginning and an end.

This is the Illusion of Insufficiency played out at the highest level.

The experience of your life beginning and ending is really nothing more than the onset and the dissolution of your idea of yourself as "separate." At a conscious level, you may not know this. At a higher level this is always clear.

It is at this higher level that you seek to end the experience of separation, to remind yourself that this is an illusion *you have created.*

Though I have told you many times, it is a good time now to discuss once more *why* you have created it.

You have created the Illusion of Disunity in order to experience the reality of Oneness. Only when you are outside the reality can you experience it. When you are part of The Whole, you cannot experience yourself *as* The Whole, because there is nothing else. And, in the absence of that which you are not, that which you are, is not.

In the absence of cold, hot is not. In the absence of tall, short is not. If everything is short, then *nothing is short,* because "short" does not exist as something that can be known. It may exist as a concept, but it is not a concept that you can directly experience. It can only be an idea, never your experienced reality.

Similarly, in the absence of Disunity, unity is not.

If everything is experienced as unified, then *nothing can be experienced as unified,* because "unity" does not exist as a discrete experience. It is not something that can be known. It may exist as a concept, but it is not a concept that you can directly experience. It can only be an idea, never your experienced reality.

In this context, you cannot know yourself as Who You Really Are.

Yet it is our wish to know ourselves as Who We Really Are. Thus, we must first create the experience of Who We Are Not. Since we cannot create this experience in Ultimate Reality, we must do so through illusion.

In this way, we can rejoice in what is really so, and know it. In this way, we can experience Who We Really Are.

The All Of It.

The One And Only.

We are The Collective, The Single Reality In Multiple Form—having *taken* Multiple Form that we might notice and experience the glory of our Single Reality.

This is a simple explanation of the purpose of relativity, which I have given you many times in our ongoing dialogue. It is repeated here so that you may understand it thoroughly, so that you may awaken from your dream.

. . .

Until you awaken from your dream, the Illusion of Disunity from Life will create a perceived need to survive. Before separation, you never questioned your survival. Only when you stepped away from Life (Me), and imagined yourself as separate, did Life Itself become that of which there was "not enough." You began to make decisions about what you felt you had to do to survive—to have more life.

This became your primary goal, your new basic instinct. You even began to think that the reason you coupled with others was to guarantee your survival as a species. You lost sight of the fact that you coupled in response to the only real instinct, which is love.

You have called your new basic instinct The Survival Instinct, based on your idea that you might *not* survive. This idea is false, for your survival is guaranteed forever, and even forevermore. Yet you do not remember this, and so do not think there is enough Life, given that there are so many aspects of life competing for it.

And, indeed, that is how you see it. You imagine that you are *in competition* with all the other "stuff of Life" for Life Itself. You are competing with your very self for more of your self. Your belief in Insufficiency has even led you to conclude that there is *not enough God.*

Not only is there not enough Life (which you translate into a belief in death), and not only is there not enough of the stuff of Life (which you translate into a belief in lack), there is not even enough of That Which Created Life (which you translate into a belief in a limited God).

Because *all of these things are limited,* you must compete for them. And you are destroying your planet and yourselves because of this belief.

You are even destroying yourselves in your competitions for God, which you call religions. You have been killing yourselves, sometimes seeking to annihilate entire civilizations, in your insane competition for God.

You do not admit that you are doing these things, because to admit it would be to acknowledge that there may be something inaccurate about the way you view life and the world— and particularly about the way you view God—and this you have not been able to do.

Such an admission would require enormous humility, and humility is not presently a large part of your planet's philosophy or theology.

Your theologies, in particular, have been most arrogant, assuming and proclaiming to have all the answers—leaving no questions and entertaining no doubts.

Yet something about these beliefs is not working. The idea that there is not enough—not enough God, not enough of the stuff of Life, not enough Life Itself—has led to more than simple competition. It has led to brutal *re*pression, to *su*ppression, and to massive *de*pression. Religions have repressed frank and honest inquiry, governments have suppressed dissent, and millions of people live, as a result, in both economic and psychological depression. All of this has come out of the idea that Insufficiency Exists—for sufficiency would solve all of this.

If you thought that there was enough to go around, there would be no more self-destructive behaviors, no more fighting over resources, no more squabbling over God.

But there is *not* enough. About this you are clear.

Still, if there is not enough, how does one *get* enough? How can survival be assured *without* killing and squabbling?

Clearly, there was a flaw in The Fourth Illusion. This should have revealed the idea of Insufficiency as false, but humans knew at some very deep level that they could not *give up* the Illusion, or something very vital would come to an end.

Again, they were right. But again, they made a mistake. Instead of seeing the Illusion *as* an illusion, and using it for the purpose for which it was intended, they thought they had to *fix the flaw.*

It was to fix the flaw in The Fourth Illusion that The Fifth Illusion was created.

5.

The Illusion of

Requirement

This is The Fifth Illusion:

The existence of Insufficiency led rapidly and inevitably to the idea of the next Illusion.

If there were enough stuff, there would be nothing you would have to do to get whatever it was that you wanted or needed. You would just reach out and it would be there. But that is not how humans decided that it is. They said, *there is not enough.* So now they faced the question: How does one *get* enough? How does one *qualify?*

You imagined that there must be something that you had to *do* in order to get the stuff of which there was not enough— something that would allow you to lay claim to it without argument. This is the only way that you could figure out how to get everything—including God—divided in your favor without killing and squabbling.

You imagined this to be the Requirement.

You told yourselves that fulfilling it—whatever it was—is "what it takes." That idea has held firm to this very day. If anything, it has grown stronger. You believe that when you do the things you need to do, you can be the things you want to be.

If you want to be happy, if you want to be secure, if you want to be loved, then there are things you are going to have to do. You cannot be these things unless you have enough. And you cannot have enough unless you do what it takes to *get* enough—to *qualify* for enough.

This is what you believe, and because you believe it, you have elevated *doing* to the highest place in your cosmology.

Even God says there is something that you have to do in order to get into heaven.

This is how you have it put together.

This is the Requirement.

Mind you, now, all of this is based on The Third Illusion—that you are separate. When there was only One of you, there was always enough, and so, there was nothing you had to do in order to be anything.

And that idea of separation was based on The Second Illusion—that Failure exists. Because God failed to get what He wanted, He separated all humans from Him.

And Failure was based on The First Illusion—that Need exists. God could not fail to get what God wanted if God wanted nothing, and God would want nothing if God needed nothing.

In truth, there is only one Illusion, and all the others are permutations of that. Everything else is an expansion of the only Illusion, with a different nuance.

Thus, the Illusion of Requirement is nothing more than a different take on the Illusion of Need. Similarly, the Illusion of Insufficiency is a different take on The Illusion of Need, as is the Illusion of Failure, and so on, through all The Illusions of Humans.

You will see very clearly, as you explore each illusion, that each is an outgrowth of the illusions that have gone before. It is like watching a balloon being blown up.

The announcement of your species that there is a Requirement that must be met in order to acquire anything of which there is not enough—including God's love—has proven to be one of the most significant decisions the human race has ever made. It has resulted in entire lists and sets of rules and regulations, guidelines and procedures, laws of God and laws of man, by which you imagine you must live your life.

Here are a few of the things you have decided that you must do in order to have a good life on earth:

Be a good boy or girl.

Don't talk back.

Get good grades and go on to college.

Graduate with a degree and find a good job.

Marry and have children.

Be good parents and give your children more than you
    were given.

Be cool.

Do as you are told.

Don't do bad things—or, at least, don't get caught.

Follow the leader.

Don't ask too many questions, and don't ask any of the wrong ones.

Keep everybody happy.

Do not include yourself in the group of people you are trying to keep happy if it may mean excluding someone else from the group.

Don't impose on anybody, especially when you get old.

And here are a few of the things you have decided that you must do in order to please God and get into heaven:

Don't do anything bad—and forget about not getting caught, because you will.

If you *do* do something bad, for God's sake, beg forgiveness and promise never, *ever* to do it again.

Be a good boy or girl.

Do not play with yourself.

Do not play with anyone else, either. Not *that* way . . .

In fact, do not play much at all. Try to understand that all pleasures of the body are, at best, distractions from what you really came to earth to do, and, at worst, absolute sins against God.

If you must have pleasures, do not enjoy them.

Do not enjoy money.

Do not enjoy attention.

Do not enjoy sex.

Above *all,* do not enjoy sex.

Never, ever, have a sexual relationship outside of marriage, and never, ever love more than one person in "that way."

If you must have sex for any reason other than procreation, be embarrassed, do not freely or uninhibitedly enjoy it.

Do not take money for something truly enjoyable, and if you make a great deal of money, make sure you give most of it away.

Believe in the right God.

For heaven's sake, *believe in the right God.*

Beg forgiveness and mercy from God for having been born imperfect, and ask Him for help in meeting the conditions for you to be loved again.

Humans have many other beliefs. These were listed here to give you just a few examples. This is what you have to do. This is the Requirement, and you would do well to understand it.

Who set this Requirement? Who put it into place?

You say that I did.

You claim that the author was God. And since there is not enough God to go around, you have to lay claim to Me in order to justify setting yourself up as the winners in your competitions.

You claim, then, that yours is the One Nation Under God, or that you are the Chosen People, or that yours is the One True Faith.

You lay claim to Me and you do so viciously, ferociously,

for you feel that if you can lay claim to Me, you can then lay claim to anything else you desire, in My name.

This you have done for centuries, waving high your holy books, your crosses, and your flags to justify taking what there is not enough of by whatever means is necessary—including killing. You have even gone so far as to call such an event a *holy war,* seeking to close wounds in your soul while you open wounds in the bodies of others.

You have performed the most ungodly acts in the name of God, and all because you think that I have a Requirement that you must fulfill in order to receive Me, My love, and all the stuff of Life.

As long as you believe there is something that you have to do, you will struggle to find out what it is, and then struggle further to achieve it.

Achievement will become your god. Indeed, it already has. Yet, if doing the right things brings you happiness and allows you to go home to God, why has all the striving to do those things felt so *un*happy, and seemed so surely to be leading you *away* from God?

And, perhaps even more important, how will it be determined whether or not all of this was worth it? By what measure, by what system, will it be decided if the Requirement has been met?

This is something you did not know. This was the question that humans began to ask.

Clearly, there was a flaw in The Fifth Illusion. This should have revealed the idea of Requirement as false, but humans knew at some very deep level that they could not *give up* the Illusion, or something very vital would come to an end.

Again, they were right. But again, they made a mistake. Instead of seeing the Illusion *as* an illusion, and using it for the purpose for which it was intended, they thought they had to *fix the flaw.*

It was to fix the flaw in The Fifth Illusion that The Sixth Illusion was created.

6.

The Illusion of

Judgment

This is The Sixth Illusion:

JUDGMENT EXISTS

Your decision that there is something that you must do in order to obtain that of which there is not enough—including God—required you to answer difficult questions: *How will it be determined whether a person has met the Requirement or not? And what will happen to those who have not?*

Your answer to these questions produced the invention of Judgment.

Someone, you reasoned, must be the final arbiter. Since the Creator was the one who established the Requirement, it seemed only logical that the Creator would also be the one to decide who had met the Requirement and who had not.

For a very long time your species has held the thought that there was something you had to do in order to please God—and that failure to please God produced dire consequences.

That you came to such a conclusion was understandable. Looking around you, you saw that some people's lives went well, and some did not. Primitive mind asked, Why? And primitive mind came up with a primitive answer:

Fortune smiled upon those who were in favor with the gods. It was the gods who had to be satisfied, and then the gods would judge.

Sacrifices and rituals of all kinds grew up around this belief, all designed to mollify difficult deities.

In these earliest days, your sense of Insufficiency was so strong that you even imagined the gods to be in competition with each other. There were many gods to please, and it was often not easy to keep track of what had to be done to keep everybody happy.

Each new earthly disaster, each hailstorm, each hurricane, each drought, or famine, or personal misfortune was seen as evidence that one of the gods had not been satisfied—or, sometimes, that they had been warring with each other.

How else to explain what was going on?

Now, these beliefs arose in ancient times, and through the millennia they have been refined and clarified. Most humans today do not believe that there is a long list of ill-tempered gods who have to be mollified. Today most people believe that there is only one ill-tempered God who has to be mollified.

And although it may seem as if your species long ago evolved out of the primitive constructions that created an "I'm-going-to-get-you" kind of God, these ideas continue to dominate your planet's theologies.

This God As Avenger model of Diety has never lost favor

in your societies. You've used both personal and planetary disasters as evidence of its validity. Even in very recent times, such as when your AIDS epidemic hit, there were many people—including some religious leaders—who proclaimed life's misfortunes to be God's punishments for the individual or collective misbehaviors of the human race.

Humans continue to agree in large numbers that there *is* a Requirement set down by Me, which they must meet in order to become eligible for rewards here and in heaven. They continue to agree that there *is* a system of Judgment by which it is determined who has met the Requirement and who has not.

On the other hand, some theologies state flatly that *no one* can meet the Requirement, no matter what they do. Not even if they lead a perfect life, without error, blunder, or mistake of any kind. This is, the teaching declares, because everyone is *born* imperfect (some religions call this Original Sin), with a blotch on their soul even before they begin.

This blotch cannot be removed by any act that the person performs, not even an act of true repentance, but only by the grace of God. And God, it is taught, will not grant this grace unless the person comes to Him in a very specific way.

This teaching claims that I am a very particular God, one who will not bestow the joys of heaven upon anyone who does not do as I say.

It is said that I am very stubborn about this; that it truly does not matter how good people may have been, how compassionate or generous or kind. It does not matter how sorry they may be for their offenses, and it does not matter what they have done to make amends. Indeed, it does not matter if they have made the greatest contribution to the betterment of life on the planet that the world has ever seen: If they have not come to Me by the right path, saying the right words, believing the right religion, they cannot sit at the right hand of God the Father Almighty.

Because such rightness is required, this idea could be called righteousness. . . .

Given their belief that this is the way God has set things up between Himself and the entire human race, members of the human race have set things up in precisely the same way with each other.

Taking a page out of God's book (what's good for Me ought, certainly, to be good for you), humans have put a "blotch" on each other even before *they* begin. As I have already described, they do this to others of the "wrong" gender, color, or religion. They extend it to those of the "wrong" nationality, neighborhood, political persuasion, sexual orientation, or whatever other "wrongness" they choose to create. In doing this, human beings "play God."

Yes, it is God, you say, who taught you to prejudge like this, for it is God who put the first blotch of imperfection on your own soul—who prejudged *you*, even before you had a chance to prove yourself, one way or the other.

Pre-judgment—that is, *prejudice*—must, therefore, be okay, for how can what is acceptable for God not be acceptable for man?

And what is the reason for My having declared all of you imperfect at the moment of your birth? I have done it, so the teaching goes, because the first humans were bad.

So we see how you have doubled back to the first three Illusions to justify the Fourth, Fifth, and Sixth. And so it is, with each Illusion producing the next, and each new Illusion proving those preceding.

Your cultural story says that when Adam and Eve sinned, they were driven from Paradise, losing happiness and their claim to eternal life—and yours along with it. This is because I sentenced them not only to a life of limitation and struggle but to eventual death (The Fourth Illusion)—none of which they experienced before they misstepped.

Other cultural stories and theologies that arose and exist on your planet do not embrace the Adam and Eve scenario but nevertheless create their own evidence of the Requirement. On this, most agree: Humans are imperfect in the eyes of God, and there is something that they have to do in order to achieve perfection—variously described as Purification, Salvation, Enlightenment . . . whatever.

Because you believe in human imperfection, and since you believe that you have received this characteristic from Me, you have felt perfectly free to pass it on to others. All the while you have expected the same thing of others that you have been told I expect of you: perfection.

And so has it come to pass that humans have gone through life demanding perfection of those whom they, themselves, have called imperfect—namely, humans.

First, they do this to themselves. This is their initial, and often most costly, error.

Then they do it to others. This is their second mistake.

They have made it impossible for either themselves *or* others to ever fully meet . . .

The Requirement.

Parents demand perfection from their imperfect children, and children demand perfection from their imperfect parents.

Citizens demand perfection from their imperfect government, and the government demands perfection from its imperfect citizens.

Churches demand perfection from their imperfect followers, and followers demand perfection from their imperfect churches.

Neighbors demand perfection from other neighbors, races from other races, nations from other nations.

You have accepted as reality the Illusion of Judgment; then you have declared that if God judges you, you have the right to judge everyone else. And judge them you do.

Your world rushes to judge, in particular, anyone receiving the rewards—fame, power, success—that are supposed to go only to the perfect, and your world condemns those in whom it uncovers the slightest imperfection.

So fanatical have you become that you have made it virtually impossible for people to become leaders, heroes, or icons in your present day and time—thus robbing yourself of exactly what your society needs.

You have placed yourself in a trap of your own devising, unable to release yourself from the Judgments you have imposed on each other, and the Judgment you believe God has imposed on you.

Yet why should a simple observation about you make you so uncomfortable? Is simply observing that something is so really a Judgment? Couldn't it be merely an observation? So what if someone has *not* met the Requirement? What does it matter?

These are the questions that humans began to ask.

Clearly, there was a flaw in The Sixth Illusion. This should have revealed the idea of Judgment as false, but humans knew at some very deep level that they could not *give up* the Illusion, or something very vital would come to an end.

Again, they were right. But again, they made a mistake. Instead of seeing the Illusion *as* an illusion, and using it for the purpose for which it was intended, they thought they had to *fix the flaw.*

It was to fix the flaw in The Sixth Illusion that The Seventh Illusion was created.

7.

The Illusion of
Condemnation

This is The Seventh Illusion:

CONDEMNATION EXISTS

There had to be a consequence of Judgment. If it was true that Judgment exists, there had to be a *why*.

Clearly, one was judged in order to determine whether one should receive the rewards of meeting the Requirement.

That's how humans constructed it. Seeking insight, trying to find answers, you went back to your original cultural stories, and to the first Illusions on which they were based.

You told yourself that I separated you from Myself when you failed to meet My Requirement the first time.

When you were perfect, you lived in a perfect world, Paradise, and you enjoyed everlasting life. Yet when you committed the Original Sin and rendered yourself imperfect, your experience of perfection in every way ended.

The most perfect thing about your perfect world was that you never died. Death did not exist. Yet with your experience of perfection ending, you accepted The Fourth Illusion as fact. Insufficiency Exists. There was not enough. There was not even enough Life.

So death must have been the _consequence._ This was the punishment for not meeting the Requirement.

But how could that be so? the advanced thinkers among you asked. Now _everybody_ dies. So, how could death be the punishment for not meeting the Requirement? Even those who _did_ meet the Requirement died!

Perhaps the reason for the existence of death was that there simply was Insufficiency in the universe. Insufficiency was the state of things. This you learned from The Fourth Illusion.

Yet if death was the result of Insufficiency, then what _was_ the outcome of not meeting the Requirement?

There was something wrong here. Something did not add up. You went back to your original myth. God threw Adam and Eve out of the garden when they did not meet the Requirement. This created Disunity, which created Insufficiency, which created the Requirement.

So Insufficiency was the result of God's punishment. The punishment was separation, and Insufficiency was the result. Death is the insufficiency of Life—so, by a stretch, death was the punishment.

This is how you reasoned it out. The purpose of death must have been to punish you for not meeting the Requirement. For without death, there was only what there always was—namely, Life Everlasting. And if you could live forever, what was the consequence of not having met God's requirement?

So what always was had to be called the reward.

That's it! you said to yourself. Everlasting Life is the _reward._ But now you had another conundrum. If death existed, then Life Everlasting could not.

Hmmm.

There's a challenge here. How to create a way for both to exist—despite the fact that the two appear to be mutually exclusive.

You decided that the death of the physical body did not mean the end of you. Since the existence of death precluded the possibility of a life that goes on forever, you decided that life must go on forever _after physical death._

But if life went on forever after physical death, then what was the point of death?

It had no point. And so, there had to be created in your _after_-death experience . . . _another outcome._

This you called Condemnation.

It fit perfectly, when you thought about it. It fell right into line with The Second Illusion—the outcome of life is in doubt; Failure Exists!

Now you could have your cake and eat it too. Now you could have death _and_ Everlasting Life, punishment _and_ reward. By placing both _after_ death, you were able to make death itself not the punishment but simply _the ultimate manifestation of Insufficiency_—the most impressive evidence of The Fourth Illusion.

One Illusion now really began to support the other. The

interweaving was perfect. Your work was complete, and this was the reality produced by your cultural story, and by your endless creation and passing on of myths that solidified it.

Myths support the Story, and the Story supports the Illusions. This is the superstructure of your entire cosmology. These are the underpinnings of all your understandings.

And they are—all of them—false.

Death does not exist. To say that death exists would be to say that you do not exist, for you are Life Itself.

To say that death exists would be to say that God does not exist, for if God is everything that is (which is exactly what God is), and if all things form a unified whole (which they do), then if one thing dies, all things die—which would mean that God dies. If one thing dies, God dies.

This, of course, cannot be. Therefore, know this: Death and God are mutually exclusive. It is not possible for them to exist side by side.

If death exists, then God does not. Or, it must be concluded that God is not everything that is.

This brings up an interesting question. Is there anything that God is not?

If you believe that there is a God, but that there is something that God is not, then you can believe in a great many other things. Not only death but the Devil, and everything in between.

If, on the other hand, you believe that God is the energy of Life Itself, and that this energy never dies but merely changes form, and that this Divine energy not only is *in* everything but is everything—that it is *the energy that forms that which has taken form*—then it is a small step to understanding that death does not, and cannot, exist.

This is what is so. I am the energy of Life. I am that which forms that which has taken form. Everything you see is God, in differing formation.

You are all God, in formation.

Or, put another way, *you are God's information.*

This I have said to you before, yet now you may at last truly comprehend it.

Much of what I have said to you in our conversations is reiterated a number of times, and this is, of course, by design. You must have a firm grasp of every concept you have been given before you can grasp new concepts you would seek to understand.

Some of you will want to move faster. Some of you will say, "Okay, I've *got it* already!" Yet do you really have it? Your life lived is a measure of what you have and what you do not have. It is a reflection of your deepest understandings.

If your life is an experience of constant joy and total bliss, then you truly have it. This does not mean that your life is without the conditions that can cause pain, suffering, and disappointment. It does mean that you live in joy *despite* those conditions. Your experience has nothing to do with conditions.

This is unconditional love, of which I have spoken many times. You may experience this with regard to another person, or with regard to Life Itself.

When you have an unconditional love of Life, then you love Life *just the way it is showing up, right here, right now.* This is possible only when you are "seeing the perfection."

I tell you that everything and everyone is perfect. When you can see this, you have taken your first step toward mastery. Yet you cannot see this unless and until you understand exactly what everyone is trying to do, and the purpose for everything under heaven.

For instance, when you understand that the purpose of this dialogue's returning to its main points repeatedly is to bring you deeper and deeper into your own understanding, and closer and closer to mastery, then you will love the repetition. You will love it because you understand the benefit. You embrace the gift.

This will bring you equanimity in this moment, and in all the moments of your life, no matter how unpleasant you might previously have judged them. You will even find equanimity in the moments before your death, for you will see your death, too, as perfect.

You will find and create equanimity even more masterfully when you understand that *every moment* is a dying. Every moment is the end of your life as what you were, and the beginning of your new life as what you now choose to become.

In each moment you are recreating yourself anew. You are either doing this consciously or unconsciously, with awareness or completely unaware of what is going on.

You do not have to be facing the moment of what you have previously called "death" in order to experience more life. You can experience more life whenever you wish, in a hundred different ways, at a hundred different times—at the moment of your birth, at the moment of your death, or at any moment in between.

This much I promise you: You *will* experience more life at the moment of your physical death—and this will do more than anything else to convince you that there *is* more life, that life goes on and on, and never, ever ends. In that instant will you realize that there was never not enough. There was never not enough of Life, and there was never not enough of the stuff of life.

This will dissolve The Fourth Illusion forever. Yet that Illusion can be dissolved *before* the moment of your death, and that is My message here.

The way to produce more life is to experience more death. Don't let death be a once-in-a-lifetime thing! Experience each moment of your life as a death, for that is, in truth, what it is when you re-define death as simply the end of one experience and the beginning of another.

When you do this, you can have a little funeral each moment for what just passed, for what just died. And then you can turn around and create the future, realizing that there *is* a future, that there is *more Life.*

When you know this, the idea of not enough is shattered, and you can begin to use each golden Moment of Now in a new way, with new understanding and deeper appreciation, with larger awareness and greater consciousness.

And your life will never be the same, ever.

· · ·

Once you understand that there is *always more Life,* you will learn to *use* the illusion that there is not enough Life in a way that serves you. This will allow the illusion to assist you, rather than hinder you, as you walk your path and make your way back home.

You can relax, because you know that you have more time, even though the illusion is that your time is running out. You can create with enormous efficiency, because you know that you have *more Life,* even though the illusion is that your life is ending. You can find peace and joy, even though the illusion is that there is not enough of whatever it is that you think you need in your life, because you know now that there *is* enough. There is enough time, there is enough Life, and there is enough of the stuff of life to allow you to live in happiness forever.

When you allow yourself to experience that there is enough of what you once thought there was *not* enough of, extraordinary changes occur in the way you live your life.

When you know that there is enough, you stop competing with others. You stop competing for love, or money, or sex, or power, or whatever it is you felt there was not enough of.

The competition is over.

This alters everything. Now, instead of competing with others to get what you want, you begin to give what you want away. Instead of fighting for more love, you begin giving more love away. Instead of struggling for success, you begin making sure that everyone else is successful. Instead of grasping for power, you begin empowering others.

Instead of seeking affection, attention, sexual satisfaction, and emotional security, you find yourself being the source of it. Indeed, everything that you have ever wanted, you are now supplying to others. And the wonder of it all is that, as you give, so do you receive. You suddenly have *more of* whatever you are giving away.

The reason for this is clear. It has nothing to do with the fact that what you have done is "morally right," or "spiritually enlightened," or the "Will of God." It has to do with a simple truth: There is no one else in the room.

There is only one of us.

Yet the Illusion says this is not so. It says that you are all separate from each other, and from Me. It says that there is not enough—not even enough of Me—and so, there is something you have to do in order to have enough. It says that you will be carefully watched to make sure that you do it. It says that if you do not do it, you will be condemned.

This does not seem to be a very loving thing to do. And yet, if there is one thing that all of your cultural stories have told you, it is that God Is Love. Supreme Love. Complete Love. Unfathomable Love. Yet if God Is Love, how could Condemnation exist? How could God sentence us to everlasting torture beyond description?

These are questions that humans began to ask.

Clearly, there was a flaw in The Seventh Illusion. This should have revealed the idea of Condemnation as false, but humans knew at some very deep level that they could not *give up* the Illusion, or something very vital would come to an end.

Again, they were right. But again, they made a mistake.

Instead of seeing the Illusion *as* an illusion, and using it for the purpose for which it was intended, they thought they had to *fix the flaw.*

It was to fix the flaw in The Seventh Illusion that The Eighth Illusion was created.

8.

The Illusion of

Conditionality

This is The Eighth Illusion:

CONDITIONALITY EXISTS

In order for Condemnation to exist, there must be something that you don't understand about love.

This was your conclusion, and you invented Conditionality as a characteristic of life in order to resolve the dilemma that this presented.

Everything in life must be conditional. Wasn't this self-evident? some of the thinkers among you asked. Have you not understood The Second Illusion? *The outcome of life is in doubt.*

Failure exists.

That means you can fail to win God's love. God's love is conditional. You must meet the Requirement. If you do not meet the Requirement, you will be separated. Is this not what The Third Illusion taught you?

Your cultural stories have been very persuasive. I have spoken in this communication largely through the stories of Western culture, because that is the culture in which this communication began. But the cultures of the East, and all of the many cultures and traditions of humans in their wide variety, have their stories as well, and most are based on some or all of The Ten Illusions.

As I have made clear, there are more than ten illusions. You are creating hundreds every day. Each of your cultures has created its own, but in some way or another they are all based on the same basic misconceptions. This is evidenced by the fact that they have all created the same results.

Life on your planet is filled with experiences of greed, violence, killing, and, nearly everywhere, conditional love.

You have learned conditional love from your thought that the love of the Supreme Being, however you conceptualize that Being, is conditional. Or, if you do not believe in a Supreme Being, but rather, in Life Itself, then you have conceived of Life as a process expressing itself within the context of Conditionality. That is to say, one condition depends upon another. Some of you would call this Cause and Effect.

Yet what of First Cause?

That is the question that none of you has been able to answer. Even your greatest scientists have not been able to unravel the mystery. Even your greatest philosophers have not been able to solve the problem.

Who created That Which Creates?

If you conceive of a cause-and-effect Universe, fair enough—but what caused the First Cause?

This is where your teachers stumble. This is where your path ends. This is where you reach the edge of understanding.

Now we shall fly off the edge.

There *is* no Conditionality in the Universe. That Which Is is That Which Is, and *there are no conditions under which It is not.*

Do you understand?

It is not possible for "What Is" not to be. There are no conditions under which that would be true. This is why Life is eternal. Because Life is That Which Is, and That Which Is can never *not be.*

Life always was, is now, and ever shall be, world without end.

So, too, with God. For God *is* what Life is.

So, too, with love. For love *is* what God is.

Love, therefore, knows no condition. Love simply is.

Love cannot not "be," and there are no conditions under which it can be made to disappear.

You may substitute the word "Life" or the word "God" for "love" in the above sentence and it would be equally true.

Conditional love is an oxymoron.

Did you get that? Do you understand that? The two are mutually exclusive. The experience of Conditionality and the experience of love cannot exist at the same time in the same place.

Your idea that they can is what is destroying you.

Your civilization has chosen to live The Eighth Illusion at

a very high level. The result is that your civilization itself is threatened with extinction.

You are not threatened with extinction. You cannot be. For you are Life Itself. Yet the form in which you express Life at the present moment—the civilization which you have created, and are about to uncreate—is not unchangeable. It is the wonder of Who You Are that you can change form whenever you wish. Indeed, you do this all the time.

If, however, you are enjoying the form in which you now experience yourself, why change it?

That is the question now facing the whole human race.

You have been given a paradise in which to live. Every possible joy of physical life has been made available to you. You are truly in a Garden of Eden. That part of your cultural Story is real. Yet you have not been separated from Me, and you never have to be. You can experience this paradise as long as you wish. Or, you can destroy it on a moment's notice.

Which do you choose?

You are about to choose the latter.

Is that your choice? Is that your conscious decision?

Look at this question very carefully. There is much riding on your answer.

The lack of true Conditionality in the Universe notwithstanding, you have believed firmly that Conditionality exists. Surely it exists in God's kingdom. Every one of your religions has taught you that. So it must exist in the Universe at large. It was, you decided, a fact of life. So you have spent lifetimes trying to figure out what conditions could allow you to create the life—and the afterlife—that you desire if you did not meet the Requirement. If you met the Requirement, there was no problem. But what if you did not?

This search has led you down a blind alley, for there *are* no conditions. You may have the life that you desire, and whatever afterlife that you imagine, *simply by choosing it.*

This you do not believe. The formula can't be that simple, you say. No, no . . . you have to meet the Requirement!

You do not understand yourselves to be creative beings. Nor do you understand Me to be so. You imagine that I can somehow fail to have something that I desire (all My children returning home to Me)—which means that I must not be a truly creative being at all but a dependent one. If I were truly creative, I would be able to create anything that I choose. But I seem to be dependent upon certain conditions in order to have what I want.

Humans could not imagine what conditions could possibly have to be met in order for them to get back home to God. So they did the best they could . . . and just *made some up.* These were explained through what you call religions.

Religions could not only explain the Requirements but could also explain how one could recapture God's love if one did not meet the Requirement. Thus, the concepts of *forgiveness* and *salvation* were born. They were the conditions of love. God says "I love you *if,*" and these were the "ifs."

Had people looked at things objectively, the fact that every religion explained forgiveness and salvation differently might have been proof that it was all being made up. But objectivity was not something humans proved to be particularly capable of. It is not something many humans are capable of even today.

You continue to declare that you are *not* making anything up. You say that the conditions of your return to God were established by Me. And if there are several hundred different religions, pointing to several thousand different conditions, it is not because I have given a mixed message, but because the human race has simply not gotten it right.

You have gotten it right, of course. It's just those *other people,* in those *other religions,* who have not gotten it right.

Now, there are a lot of ways you could solve that. You could ignore them. You could try to convert them. You could even decide to simply eliminate them.

Your race has tried all of those things. And you had a right to do so, didn't you? You had a responsibility to do so, didn't you? Was this not the work of God? Were you not called upon to convince and convert others so that they, too, might know what was right? And was your killing and your ethnic cleansing not justified when others could not be convinced? Was there not something, some unwritten "something," that gave you this right?

These are questions that humans began to ask.

Clearly, there was a flaw in The Eighth Illusion. This should have revealed the idea of Conditionality as false, but humans knew at some very deep level that they could not *give up* the Illusion, or something very vital would come to an end.

Again, they were right. But again, they made a mistake.

Instead of seeing the Illusion *as* an Illusion, and using it for the purpose for which it was intended, they thought they had to *fix the flaw.*

It was to fix the flaw in The Eighth Illusion that The Ninth Illusion was created.

9.

The Illusion of
Superiority

This is The Ninth Illusion:

SUPERIORITY EXISTS

Humans concluded that if Conditionality existed, then *knowing* the conditions would be necessary to enjoy and create the life—and the afterlife—that one desired.

This conclusion was unavoidable, as was: Those who knew the conditions were better off than those who did not.

And it did not take much time for the human race to remove the word "off" from the previous sentence.

Thus the idea of Superiority was born.

Superiority had many uses. Chief among them was providing inarguable justification for doing whatever was needed in order to guarantee that "enough" of everything—including God's love—was available. Knowing the conditions gave one the right to ignore others, or seek to convert others, or simply eliminate others who did not know the conditions, or agree to them.

Therefore, seeking to know the conditions of Life became a major preoccupation. Knowing the conditions of Life was called science. Knowing the conditions of the afterlife was called conscience. If one knew these conditions and understood them, one was said to have "a good conscience," or to be "conscious."

A "high consciousness" was said to result from the earnest study of something you called theology, from theo + logy, or, loosely, God logic.

After much study, it was concluded that there were certain circumstances under which the Requirement could be met, and certain circumstances under which that was impossible. There were also certain circumstances under which one could be forgiven for *not* having met the Requirement.

These circumstances came to be known as "the conditions."

"Having" was added to "doing" in your experience.

When you have enough brains, you can do the thing called get good grades, graduate at the top of your class, and find a great job. Then you can be the thing called successful.

When you have enough money, you can do the thing called buy a wonderful house, and you can be the thing called secure.

When you have enough time, you can do the thing called take a vacation, and you can be the thing called rested, refreshed, and relaxed.

When you have enough power, you can do the thing called determine your own destiny, and you can be the thing called free.

When you have enough faith, you can do the thing called find God, and you can be the thing called saved.

This is how you set up your world. When someone has the right stuff, they can do the right things—the things that allow them to be what they've always wanted to be.

The difficulty is that people cannot easily *do* all the things they need to *do* unless they have all of the things you say they need to have.

They cannot get a good job and rise to the top, even if they have the brains, unless they are also the right gender. They cannot buy a wonderful house even if they have the money, unless they also have the right skin color. They cannot find God, even if they have faith, unless they also have the right religious beliefs.

Having the right stuff is not a guarantee of getting all that you desire, but it gives you a big head start.

The more knowledge of these conditions one acquired (or was thought to have acquired), the more superior one was understood to be. As has been mentioned, this Superiority gave people the authority (or encouraged people to grant themselves the authority) to do whatever they felt was necessary in order to assure themselves more Life and more God—neither of which there was enough of.

This is why you've had to do what you've had to do: because there was not enough. This is what you have told yourself. Your entire species has accepted this mantra.

There's more than one of you, and so there is not enough to go around. Not enough food, not enough money, not enough love, not enough God.

You have to compete for it.

And if you're going to compete, you have to have some way of figuring out who wins.

Superiority was your answer.

The one who is superior wins—and Superiority is based on certain conditions.

Some humans sought to guarantee that they would win, and so arbitrarily added to the conditions. They made it possible to declare themselves the victors in advance.

They declared, for instance, that males were superior to females. Wasn't this self-evident? some of the thinkers among you asked. (Of course, it was mostly males doing the asking.)

Similarly, whites were pronounced to be Superior.

And then, later, Americans.

And, of course, Christians.

Or was it Russians? And Jews? Or women?

Could such things be true? Of course they could. It all depended upon *who was creating the system.*

The very earliest superior beings were not male . . . and males actually agreed. After all, were females not the bringers of life? And was life not that for which everyone had the highest desire? So it was during your matriarchal period that females were considered superior.

Similarly, the white race was not the first race, and therefore not superior.

In *truth,* it is not superior today.

Nor are males superior.

Nor Jews.

Nor Christians.

Nor Muslims, Buddhists, Hindus, nor even Democrats or Republicans, Conservatives or Communists, nor *anything else whatsoever.*

Here is the truth—the truth that will set you free, the truth you cannot allow to be spoken because it *will* set everyone free:

There is no such thing as Superiority.

You have *made it all up.*

You have defined what *you* think is superior, based on your preferences and your desires and your understandings (which are very limited, indeed). You have announced what you proclaim to be better based on *your* perspective and *your* objectives and *your* agenda.

Yet some of you have claimed this is *My* agenda. *God* is the one who named the Chosen People, or the One True Faith, or the only path to salvation.

All of this goes back to The First Illusion: Need Exists.

You imagine that because God has needs, that God has an agenda.

This was your first mistake, and it has led to what could be your last. For I tell you this: Your idea of Superiority could be the last mistake you ever make.

Humans think that they are superior to nature, and so, they seek to subdue it. In doing this, they destroy the very habitat which was created to protect them and to be their paradise.

Humans think that they are superior to each other, and so, they seek to subdue each other. In doing this, they destroy the very family that was created to embrace them and to give them love.

Your species is making it very difficult to experience Life in its present form because of your belief in the Illusions. By not using the Illusions as they were intended, you are turning what was intended to be a beautiful dream into a living nightmare.

But you can undo all of this right now. Simply see the Illusions for what they are—realities contrived for a purpose—and then stop living them as if they were real.

In particular, stop living The Ninth Illusion with such conviction. Indeed, use the Illusion to notice that Superiority is not real. There can be no such thing as Superiority when We Are All One. A thing cannot be superior to itself.

All things are One Thing, and there is nothing else. "We Are All One" is more than a beautiful slogan. *It is a precise description of the nature of Ultimate Reality.* When you understand this, you begin experiencing life—and treating each other—in a new way. You see the relationship of all things differently. You notice the connectedness at a much higher level. Your awareness is expanded, your insight becomes very keen. You, quite literally, *see in.*

This increased ability to peer deeply into life allows you to look past the Illusion and to recognize—to "know again," to re-*cognize*—*your* reality. It is by this process that you re-member Who You Really Are.

This movement, from not knowing to knowing again, may be made slowly. The journey may be undertaken in small steps. Small steps can produce large advances. Always remember that.

One such small step would be to put an end to better.

The idea of Superiority is the most seductive idea ever visited upon the human race. It can turn the heart to stone, change warm to cold, yes to no, in an instant.

A single sentence, uttered from your pulpits, lecterns, and rostrums, by your national congresses and your world summit leaders, could change everything.

"Ours is not a better way, ours is merely another way."

This humble utterance could begin to heal the divisions between your religions, close the gap between your political parties, curb the conflicts between your nations.

With one *word* you could end them.

"Namasté."

God in me honors God in you.

How simple. How beautiful. How wondrous, indeed.

Yet how difficult, when one is caught up in the Illusion, to see God in every one and every thing. Each person would have to be aware of the Illusion—be aware that it *is* an illusion.

Yet if it is not an illusion but is life as it really is, then how is it that precisely when we imagine ourselves to be superior, we behave in the most inferior ways? Why is it that it is exactly when we think ourselves better that we act worse?

Clearly, there was a flaw in The Ninth Illusion. This should have revealed the idea of Superiority as false, but humans knew at some very deep level that they could not *give up* the Illusion, or something very vital would come to an end.

Again, they were right. But again, they made a mistake.

Instead of seeing the Illusion *as* an illusion, and using it for the purpose for which it was intended, they thought they had to *fix the flaw.*

It was to fix the flaw in The Ninth Illusion that The Tenth Illusion was created.

10.

The Illusion of
Ignorance

This is The Tenth Illusion:

IGNORANCE EXISTS

Increasingly, as each Illusion was piled upon the last, Life became more and more difficult to figure out. Humans asked more and more questions that could not be answered. If this was true, then why that? If that was true, then why this? It wasn't long before philosophers and teachers began throwing up their hands. "We don't know," they said, "and we don't know if it's *possible* to know."

Thus, the idea of Ignorance was born.

This idea served so many purposes that it spread quickly and soon became the ultimate answer.

We just don't know.

Human institutions began finding in this not only a refuge but a certain kind of power. "We don't know" turned into "we are not *supposed* to know," which became "you do not have a *need* to know," which finally became "what you don't know won't hurt you."

This gave religions and governments the authority to say what they chose, and act as they pleased, without having to answer to anyone.

"We are not supposed to know" actually became a religious doctrine. There are certain secrets of the Universe that God does not want us to know, this doctrine declared, and to even inquire about such things was blasphemy. This doctrine quickly spread from religion to politics and government.

The result: There was a time in your history when certain questions asked at certain times in certain ways could get one's head cut off.

Literally.

This prohibition against inquiry elevated Ignorance to a desirable attribute. It became very wise and very good manners not to ask questions. It became accepted behavior. Indeed, *expected* behavior.

And while the punishment for the offense of impertinent inquiry may not seem quite as severe today as it was in days gone by, there are certain places on your planet where little has changed.

Certain totalitarian regimes insist to this very hour that only voices of agreement be heard and that voices of dissent be silenced, sometimes in the most brutal ways.

Such barbaric behaviors are justified by proclamations that they are "necessary to ensure order." Protests by the international community are met with indignant sniffs, repressive governments declaring such issues "internal matters."

Now I tell you this: The essence of love is freedom. Anyone who says they love you, and that they are looking out for you, will grant you freedom.

It is as simple as that. You do not have to look further or deeper for more sophisticated understanding.

I have told you before, and I will tell you again. There are only two energies at the core of the human experience: love and fear.

Love grants freedom, fear takes it away. Love opens up, fear closes down. Love invites full expression, fear punishes it.

By this measure you can know whether someone is loving you, or fearing you. Do not look to what they say. Look to what they do.

Love invites you, always, to break the bonds of ignorance. To ask any question. To seek any answer. To speak any word. To share any thought. To support any system. To worship any God.

To live your truth.

Love invites you, always, *to live your truth.*

That's how you can know that it is love.

I love you. That is why I have come to tell you that *Ignorance is an Illusion.*

You know everything that there is to know about Who You Really Are—which is the essence of love. There is nothing you have to learn. You need merely remember.

You have been told that you cannot know God, and that to even ask about Me is an offense against Me.

That is not true.

Neither of those statements is true.

You have been told that there is something that I need

from you, and if you do not give it to Me, you may not return Home, to Oneness with Me.

That is not true.

Neither of those statements is true.

You have been told that you are separate from Me, and that you are separate from each other.

That is not true.

Neither of those statements is true.

You have been told that there is not enough, and that you must therefore compete with each other for everything, including Me.

That is not true.

Neither of those statements is true.

You have been told that if you do not do what I require in this competition, you will be punished, and that the punishment is condemnation to everlasting torture.

That is not true.

Neither of those statements is true.

You have been told that My love for you is conditional, and that if you know and meet My conditions, and all the conditions needed to win the competition for life, then you are superior.

That is not true.

Neither of those statements is true.

Finally, you have been told that *you do not know* that these statements are untrue, and that you can *never* know, because it is all far too much for you to understand.

That is not true.

Neither of those statements is true.

NOW HERE IS THE TRUTH . . .

1. God needs nothing.
2. God cannot fail, and neither can you.
3. Nothing is separate from anything.
4. There is enough.
5. There is nothing you have to do.
6. You will never be judged.
7. You will never be condemned.
8. Love knows no condition.
9. A thing cannot be superior to itself.
10. You already know all of this.

PART II

Mastering the Illusions

11.

Teaching Your Children Well

Teach these truths to your children.

Teach your children that they need nothing exterior to themselves to be happy—no person, place, or thing—and that true happiness is found within. Teach them that they are *sufficient unto themselves.*

Teach them this, and you will have taught them grandly.

Teach your children that failure is a fiction, that every trying is a success, and that every effort is what achieves the victory, with the first no less honorable than the last.

Teach them this, and you will have taught them grandly.

Teach your children that they are deeply connected to all of Life, that they are One with all people, and that they are never separate from God.

Teach them this, and you will have taught them grandly.

Teach your children that they live in a world of magnificent abundance, that there is enough for everyone, and that it is in *sharing* the most, not in *gathering* the most, that the most is received.

Teach them this, and you will have taught them grandly.

Teach your children that there is nothing that they are required to be or to do to be eligible for a life of dignity and fulfillment, that they need not compete with anyone for anything, and that God's blessings are meant for everyone.

Teach them this, and you will have taught them grandly.

Teach your children that they will never be judged, that they need not worry about always getting it right, and that they do not have to change anything, or "get better," to be seen as perfect and beautiful in the eyes of God.

Teach them this, and you will have taught them grandly.

Teach your children that consequences and punishment are not the same thing, that death does not exist, and that God would never condemn anyone.

Teach them this, and you will have taught them grandly.

Teach your children that there are no conditions to love, that they need not worry about ever losing your love, or God's, and that their own love, unconditionally shared, is the greatest gift they can give to the world.

Teach them this, and you will have taught them grandly.

Teach your children that being special does not mean being better, that claiming superiority over someone is not seeing them for Who They Really Are, and that there is great healing in acknowledging "mine is not a better way, mine is merely another way."

Teach them this, and you will have taught them grandly.

Teach your children that there is nothing that they cannot do, that the illusion of Ignorance can be eradicated from the earth, and that all anyone really needs is to be given back to themselves by being reminded of Who They Really Are.

Teach them this, and you will have taught them grandly.

Teach these things not with your words but with your actions; not with discussion but with demonstration. For it is what you do that your children will emulate, and how you are that they will become.

Go now and teach these things not only to your children but to all people and all nations. For all people are your children, and all nations are your home, when you set out on the journey to mastery.

This is the journey on which you embarked many centuries and many lifetimes ago. It is the journey for which you have long prepared and that has brought you here, to this time and place.

This is the journey that calls you more urgently now than ever before, on which you feel yourself proceeding with ever-increasing speed.

This is the inevitable outcome of the yearning of your soul. It is the speaking of your heart, in the language of your body. It is the expression of Divinity within you. And it calls to you now as it has never called before—because you are hearing it now as it was never heard before.

It is time to share with the world a glorious vision. It is the vision of all minds that have ever truly searched, of all hearts that have ever truly loved, of all souls that have ever truly felt the Oneness of Life.

Once you have felt this, you can never be satisfied with anything less. Once you have experienced it, you will want nothing but to share it with all those whose lives you touch.

For this is the Reality, and it stands in spectacular contrast to the Illusion. You will be able to experience the Reality, and to know it, *because* of the Illusion. Yet you are not the Illusion, and the "you" that you experience within the Illusion is not Who You Really Are.

You cannot remember Who You Really Are as long as you imagine the Illusion to be real. You must understand that the Illusion is an illusion—that you created it, for purposes very real, but that the Illusion itself is not real.

This is what you have come here to remember, with more clarity than you have ever remembered it before.

The transformation of your world will depend on your re-membering. The meaning of the word *education* is not "to put in," but "to draw out." All true education is the drawing out from the student of what is already there. The Master knows that it is already there and has no need, therefore, to place it there. The Master simply endeavors to cause *the student* to notice that it is there.

Teaching is never about helping others to learn but about helping them to remember.

All learning is remembering. All teaching is reminding. All lessons are memories, recaptured.

It is impossible to teach something new, for there is nothing new to teach. Everything that ever was, is now, and ever shall be, *is, right now.*

The soul has access to all of this information. Indeed, the soul *is* all of this . . . *in formation.*

The soul is the Body of God, in formation.

I am in a constant process of formation. That process has been called evolution, and it is a process that never ends.

If you think of God as a process, or a being, that is "finished," you have not correctly remembered what is so. Here is a great secret: *God is never finished.*

With anything. Including you.

God is never finished with you.

That is because *you* are what *God* is. And since God is not finished with God, God cannot possibly be finished with you.

Now, here is the Divine dichotomy: I have said that everything that ever was, is now, and ever shall be, *is,* right now. I have also said that the process of evolution is never-ending, and, thus, never over. How can both be true?

The answer has to do with the nature of time, as you understand it. In truth, there is no such thing as time, there is simply a process which is going on continually in the never-ending Moment of Now.

God is a process.

It is not possible for you to understand this within the framework of human logic or the limitations of the human mind. These limitations are self-imposed, and they are self-imposed for a reason. It goes back to the reason for the entire Illusion, which has been explained to you many times now—and will be explained one more time before this present communication comes to an end.

For now, simply know that God is never done "Godding." The process by which I experience Myself is ongoing, never-ending, and instant.

The particular aspect of Me that is manifesting as human life on earth is even now being transformed. You are, in these present days and times, choosing to play a conscious role in this transformation. Your choice to play that role is demonstrated by the simple act of picking up this book. You would not have done so—much less read this far—without having an intention at some very deep level to return to awareness.

Even if you imagine yourself to be reading this book as a skeptic or a critic, that is just your current imagining. Your underlying purpose in having come to this communication is to bring about a grand remembering.

This remembering is what is occurring now all over your world, throughout your human society. It has begun in earnest, and you can see evidence of it all around you.

You are nearing the second stage of the process of transforming life on your planet, and it can be complete in a very short period of time—a few decades, one or two generations—if you choose.

The first stage of this transformation has taken much longer—indeed, several thousand years. But even this, in cosmic terms, is a very short time. It is during this period of the awakening of humanity that individuals whom you have called teacher, Master, guru, or avatar undertook the task of reminding others of Who They Really Are.

As the number of people who are touched by this early group and their teaching increases to critical mass, you will experience a quickening of the spirit, or what you might call a breakthrough, in which second-stage transformation begins.

Now the adults begin teaching their young—and from that point, the movement is very fast.

Your race is at this breakthrough point now. Many humans felt a shift when you moved into your new millennium.

This was a key point in the onset of a global shift of consciousness in which you are now playing your role.

The key to continuing this momentum lies with your young. If the education of your offspring now includes certain life principles, your species can make the quantum leap forward in its evolution of which it is capable.

Build your schools around concepts, not academic subjects: core concepts such as awareness, honesty, responsibility; subtopics such as transparency, sharing, freedom, full self-expression, joyous sexual celebration, human bonding, and diversity in oneness.

Teach your children these things, and you will have taught them grandly. Above all, teach them of the Illusion, and how—and why—to live *with* it, and not *within* it.

12.

Seeing the Illusions
as illusions

How can you see the Illusion *as* an illusion when it appears to be so real? And how is it that it seems so real if it *is* an illusion?

These are the questions humans are beginning to ask as your species moves into the experience of its own conscious evolution. Now there will be answers, and you will step out of the Illusion of Ignorance.

I will give you answers here, for your consideration.

Remember, *as with all communications from God,* take what you read as valuable, but not as infallible. Know that you are your own highest authority. Whether you read the Talmud or the Bible, the Bhagavad Gita or the Qur'an, the Pali Canon or the Book of Mormon, or any holy text, do not place your source of authority outside of you. But, rather, *go within* to see if the truth you've found is in harmony with the truth you find in your heart. If it is, do not say to others, "This book is true." Say, "This book is true for me."

And if others ask you about the way you are living because of the truth you have found within you, be sure to say that yours is not a better way, yours is merely another way.

For that is what this present communication is. *This communication is just another way of looking at things.* If it makes the world more clear for you, fine. If it puts you more closely in touch with your own innermost truth, good. But be careful not to turn this into your new "holy scripture," for then you will have simply replaced one set of beliefs with another.

Seek not a set of beliefs, seek an awareness of what you know. Use whatever you find that returns you to that awareness. Understand that you are living an illusion, and that none of it is real. Yet the Illusion *points* to what is real and can give you an experience of it.

How can you see the Illusion *as* an illusion when it appears to be so real? And how is it that it seems so real if it *is* an Illusion?

The second question will be answered first.

The Illusion seems so real because so many people believe that it is not *an illusion.*

In your Alice in Wonderland world, everything is as you believe it to be. There are thousands, millions, of examples of that. Here are two.

Once, you believed that the sun revolved around the earth—and, indeed, for you it did. All of your evidence *proved that it did!* So certain were you of this truth that you developed an entire science of astronomy around it.

Once, you believed that everything physical moved from one point to another through time and space. All of your evidence *proved it!* So certain were you of this truth that you built an entire system of physics around it.

Now listen carefully. The wonder of these sciences and these systems *is that they worked.*

The astronomy that you created based on your belief that the earth was the center of the Universe *worked* to explain the visual phenomena you saw in the movement of the planets across the night sky. Your observations supported your belief, creating what you called knowledge.

The physics that you created based on your belief about particles of matter *worked* to explain the visual phenomena you saw in the physical world. Again, your observations supported your belief, creating what you called knowledge.

Only later, when you looked more closely at what you were seeing, did you change your mind about these things. Yet that change of mind did not come easily. The first people who suggested such a change of mind were called heretics or, in later times, foolish or mistaken. Their ideas of a new astronomy, with the earth revolving around the sun, or of quantum physics, in which particles of matter did not move in a continuous line through time and space but were seen to *disappear* in one place and *reappear in another,* were labeled spiritual and scientific blasphemy. Their proponents were discouraged, denounced, even put to death for their beliefs.

It is *your* beliefs that were true, the majority of you insisted. After all, were they not supported by every observation? Yet, which came first, the belief or the observation? That is the central question. That is the inquiry you did not wish to make.

Is it possible that you see what you want to see? Could it be that you observe what you expect to observe? Or perhaps more to the point, *looked right past* what you do *not expect to observe?*

I tell you, the answer is yes.

Even today, when your modern science—tired of the mistakes of the past—vows to observe *first,* and draw conclusions *later,* still those conclusions cannot be trusted. That is because it is impossible for you to look at anything objectively.

Science has concluded that *nothing which is observed is unaffected by the observer.* Spirituality told you this centuries ago, and now science has caught up. Your doctors and laboratories have learned that they must conduct double-blind tests during important research to even come close to guaranteeing accuracy.

In human experience, all things are considered within the context of what you think you already understand. You cannot help but do this. You know no other way to proceed.

Put another way, you are looking at the Illusion from within the Illusion.

Every conclusion you come to about the Illusion is, therefore, *based on* the Illusion. And so, every conclusion is an illusion.

Let this be your new insight and your constant reminder: *Every conclusion is an illusion.*

Now, let us return to the first question. How can you recognize the Illusion as an illusion when it seems so real?

You have just learned that the reason it seems so real is not because it *is* real, but because you *believe* so firmly that it is. Therefore, to change the way you see the Illusion, change what you believe about it.

In the past, you were told that seeing is believing. But lately a new idea has been advanced—that *believing is seeing*. And I tell you, this is true.

If, when you confront the Illusion, you *believe* it is an illusion, you will *see* it as an illusion, even though it seems very real. You will then be able to *use the Illusion as it was intended to be used*—as a tool with which to experience Ultimate Reality.

You will remember to create the Illusion. You will cause it to be what you *wish* it to be, rather than simply watching it present itself as you think that it *has* to be, out of your agreement that "that's just the way it is."

So just how can you do this?

You are already doing it. You simply do not know it and are thus making unconscious, rather than conscious, choices. That is, when you are making true choices at all. Most of the time you are simply accepting the choices of others.

Your choice has been to choose what others have chosen. And so, you re-live the cultural story of your forebears—as they did of theirs, even unto the seventh generation.

The day that you stop choosing what has been chosen *for* you will be the moment of your liberation.

You will not then *escape* the Illusion but be liberated from it. You will step outside of the Illusion, but will continue to live with it, free of its ability to control you or your reality.

You will never choose to end the Illusion, once you understand its purpose, until your own purpose is fulfilled.

Your purpose is not only to know and experience Who You Really Are, but to *create* Who You Next Will Be. It is your function to re-create yourself anew in every single Moment of

Now, in the next grandest version of the greatest vision you ever held about Who You Are. *This* is the process you have called evolution.

Yet you need not be affected by this process in any negative way. You can be in this world but not of it.

When you are, you will begin to experience the world as you choose to experience it. You will then understand experience itself to be an *action* rather than a *reaction;* something that you are *making,* not something that you are *having.*

When you understand this, everything in your life will change. When *enough* of you understand this, everything on your *planet* will change.

Those who *have* understood this secret have been called Masters. Those who have taught this secret have been called avatars. Those who have lived this secret have been called blesséd.

Therefore, blesséd be.

To live as an enlightened Master, you must become a heretic and a blasphemer, for you will not believe what everyone else believes, and others will deny your new truth even as you deny their old one.

You will deny that the world as others are experiencing it is real, as did those who denied that the world was flat. As in those days, this will fly in the face of what seems incontrovertible, based on the appearance of things. As in those days, this will generate argument and disagreement, and you will set sail across stormy oceans to discover endless horizons. And, as in those days, you will live in a new world.

This is the world that you have been waiting to create, and which you have been meant to experience, from the beginning of time. Time, too, is an illusion, so it might more correctly be said "since the Illusion began."

Always remember: The Illusion is not something you are enduring, it is something you are choosing.

You do not have to live the Illusion if you do not choose to.

You are here because you wish to be. If you did not so wish, it would not so be.

Yet know that the Illusion in which you live is being created *by* you, not *for* you by someone else.

Human beings who do not wish to take responsibility for the life they are experiencing say that God has created it, and that they have no choice except to endure it.

Yet I tell you that the world you live in is the way it is because that is the way you have chosen it to be. When you no longer wish the world to be the way it is, you will change it.

This is a truth that not many humans can accept. Because to accept it they would have to acknowledge their complicity, and this is something they cannot bring themselves to do. They would rather cast themselves in the role of unwilling victim than of unwitting co-creator.

This is understandable, of course. You could not forgive yourself if you thought that your world was the product of your own creation, the result of your own wills and desires. And why could you not forgive yourself? *Because you do not think that I would forgive you.*

You have been taught that there is such a thing as "the unforgivable." And how can you forgive yourself for something that you know will not be forgiven by God? You cannot. And so you do the next best thing. *You excuse yourself from having had anything to do with it.* You deny responsibility for what you imagine that I would call the inexcusable sins of man.

This is tortured logic, because if you did not create the world as it is, then who did? If someone says that God created all the horrible flaws in the world, you jump to defend Me. "No, no, no," you say. "God merely gave man free will. It is man who has created these things."

Yet if I say, "You are *right*. I did *not* create, and I *do not* create, your life as it is. *You* are the creator of your reality," you deny that, too.

Thus, you seek to have it both ways. God did not create these things, and you did not create these things. We are both merely sadly observing them.

But when you become really angry or frustrated with life, some of you change your tune. When things get bad enough, you are ready to blame Me after all.

"How can you let this happen?" you call out to Me. Some of you even shake your fist at the heavens.

The Illusion has turned to confusion. Not only is the world a cruel place, it has been *created* that way by a cruel and heartless God.

To sustain this thought, you must see yourself as separate from God, since creating a cruel and heartless world is not something that you would do. You must imagine a God who would do what you would never do, and you must see yourself as subject to His whim.

This you have done—religiously.

Still, even in this you see a contradiction, for the God of your *highest* understanding, also, would not do these things. So who *did* do them? Who *is* doing them to this very day? *Somebody* must be responsible, so *who is it?*

Enter Satan.

To resolve the contradiction of a loving God who would do unloving things, and to escape your own responsibility in this matter, you have created a third party.

The perfect scapegoat.

The Devil.

Now, at last, everything is understandable. There is Another, who stands between what you want and what I want, and who makes us both miserable.

You are not responsible for the uncaring, unloving world in which you live. You did not create it.

"Well," you might say, "maybe at some level I did create it, but it was not my fault. The Devil made me do it."

A comedian's line has become your theology.

Or is it that your theology has become a comedian's line?

Only you can decide.

13.

Understanding the Purpose of the Illusions

There is a way to end the confusion, there is a way to see the Illusion *as* an illusion, and that is to *use* the Illusion.

You will know that the Illusion is not real when you see that you can easily manipulate it.

You may claim that you cannot do this. You may say that this is a big order, more than you are up to. Yet humans consciously create illusions every day, and live within them.

Do you know anyone who sets his clock or watch ahead fifteen minutes in order to never be late?

There are those on your planet who do this! They actually set their clock or their watch five or ten or fifteen minutes ahead of the time that it actually is. Then when they look to see what time it is, they motivate themselves to hurry up, because they are pretending that it is several minutes later than it really is.

Some people actually forget that they are playing this little trick on themselves, and think that it really is the time that it is not. *This is when the Illusion no longer serves them. It does not serve its intended purpose.*

The person who understands that the time on his watch is an illusion that *he has created himself* relaxes when he sees the time, because he knows that he has a few more minutes. He goes into high gear and becomes very efficient, precisely because he *is* relaxed. He understands that the Illusion is not the reality.

The person who has temporarily forgotten that the time on his watch is an illusion, and one that *he has created himself,* is filled with anxiety because *he thinks that the Illusion is real.*

Thus, two people have two entirely different reactions to the same circumstance. One experiences the illusion as an illusion, and the other experiences it as reality.

Only when an Illusion is recognized as an illusion and *lived* as an illusion can it lead to an experience of Ultimate Reality. Then it serves the purpose of its creator.

You now understand much better.

The way to use the Illusion is to know that it *is* an illusion, and the way to know that it *is* an Illusion is to use it. The process is circular, like Life Itself.

It begins with your denial of the Illusion as having anything to do with reality. For a very long time you have been denying Ultimate Reality. You have been denying Who I Am, and Who You Really Are. *Now you will simply turn your denial around.*

You might call this denial "reversal."

Look around you and make a simple declaration: *Nothing in my world is real.*

It is that simple.

I have told you this before, in many ways at many times. I am telling it to you again, here.

Nothing that you see is real.

It is your watch, set ahead ten minutes.

You are actually "watching yourself." That is, you are deluding yourself into thinking that what is not so, is so.

But you must watch out, because you can forget very easily that *you are living within an illusion of your own creation.*

Some of you may feel depressed when you are told that what you are experiencing on your planet is all make-believe. Yet do not be downhearted, for your world is your greatest gift, a wonder for you to behold, a treasure for you to enjoy.

Life in the physical realm is glorious, indeed, and its purpose is to bring you happiness through the awareness and the declaration, the expression and the fulfillment, of Who You Really Are. Go, therefore, into this magnificent world of your creation, and make of your lifetime an extraordinary statement and a breathtaking experience of the most glorious idea that you have ever had about your self.

Remember that every act is an act of self-definition. Every thought carries the energy of creation. Every word is a declaration of what is true for you.

Look to see what you are doing today. Is this how you choose to define yourself?

Look to see what you are thinking today. Is this what you wish to create?

Look to see what you are saying today. Is this what you desire to be so?

Each moment of your life is a holy moment, a moment of creation. Each moment is a new beginning. In each, you are born again.

This is your journey to mastery. It is a journey that will lead you out of the nightmare of your own construction and into that wondrous dream which your life was intended to be. It is a journey that will lead you to your meeting with the Creator.

14.

Meditating on
the Illusions

It has been said here that when human beings reach mastery, nothing makes them unhappy. It has also been said that there is a great secret that allows Masters to be in this place.

I have already told you this secret but did not identify it as "the secret." And so you may not have understood that this insight was the key to everything.

Here is the insight again. Here is the secret.

Disunity does not exist.

This insight can change your entire experience of life. This insight translates into a simple statement that, if lived as your day-to-day reality, would turn your world upside down:

We Are All One.

What this would *really* do is turn your world right side up! For when you realize that there is One Thing, and only One Thing, One reality and only One reality, One Being and only One Being, then you comprehend that, at some level, the One Being is—and must be—*always getting Its way.*

In other words, *Failure does not exist.*

And when you reach this level of clarity, you also see clearly that in the absence of failure, the one Being is without nothing.

Therefore, *Need does not exist.*

Suddenly, with enlightenment, the dominoes fall backward. The construction of your illusions caves in upon itself. It is not the Illusions themselves that crumble, but the constructions they support. That is, the cultural stories upon which you have built your life.

These stories have all been myths—from the story of what you imagine it takes to make your life work right here and right now, to the story of how you imagine that it all began—having nothing to do with Ultimate Reality.

For you to advance now in your evolution as a species, there must be a disconnect from these stories. And disconnection can be accomplished in a number of ways. The most effective of these is stillness.

In the stillness, you will find your true being. In the silence you will hear the breathing of your soul—and of God.

I have told you many times, and I tell you here again: You will find Me in the stillness.

Meditate every day. Ask yourself: Can you give fifteen minutes each morning and fifteen minutes each evening to God?

If you cannot, if you do not have the time, if your schedule is too busy, if there is just too much else that you have to do, then you have been caught up in the Maya, in the Illusion, more deeply than even you may have thought.

Yet it is not too late—it is never too late—to step away from the Illusion, see it for what it is, and use it to allow yourself to experience the Ultimate Reality of Who You Really Are.

Begin by setting aside a tiny percentage of your waking hours each day—that is all it will take—to commune once more with Me.

I am calling you into communion with God. I am inviting you to experience your meeting with the Creator.

In that moment of communion, you will know that Unity is the truth of your being. And when you come out of your meditation, you will understand, and see from your experience, that it is the denial of this truth that perpetuates the negative effects of the Illusion.

The Illusion was meant to be your joy. It was meant to be your tool. It was never intended to be your burden and your sorrow, your trial and tribulation. And it will cease to be so when you understand the Ultimate Reality: *There is no separation.*

There is no separation *of* anything, *from* anything. There is only Unity. There is only Oneness.

You are not separate from each other, nor from any part of Life. Nor from Me.

Because Disunity does not exist, Insufficiency *can* not. For The One That *Is* is sufficient unto Itself.

Because Insufficiency does not exist, Requirement cannot.

For when there is nothing you need, there is nothing that you have to do to acquire anything.

Because there is nothing that you have to do, you will not be judged by whether you have done it or not.

Because you will not be judged, you cannot be condemned.

Because you will never be condemned, you will know at last that love is unconditional.

Because love is unconditional, there is no one and no thing that is superior in God's kingdom. There are no rankings, or hierarchies, there are not some who are loved more than others. Love is an experience total and complete. It is not possible to love a little, or to love a lot. Love is not quantifiable. One can love in different ways but not to different degrees.

Always remember that.

Love is not quantifiable.

It is either present or it is not, and in God's kingdom love is always present. That is because God is not the *dispenser* of love, God *Is* Love.

Now I have said that you and I are One, and that is what is so. You are made in My image and likeness. Therefore, you, too, are love. In a word, that is Who You Really Are. You are not the receiver of love, you are that which you would seek to receive. This is a great secret, and knowing this secret changes people's lives.

People spend whole lifetimes seeking that which they already have. They have it, because they *are it.*

All you have to do to have love is to be love.

You are My beloved. Each of you. All of you. None of you is more lovable than another, because none of you is *more of Me* than another—although some of you remember more of Me, and, therefore, more of yourself.

So do not forget yourself.

Beloved, be love.

Do this in remembrance of Me.

For you are all a part of Me, a member of the Body of God. And when you remember Who You Really Are, you are doing that quite literally. That is, you are re-*membering*— becoming a member once again of the One Body.

There is only One Body.

One Being.

Always remember that.

Because there is no Superiority, there are not some who know more than others, and some who know less. There are merely those who remember more, and remember less, of what has always been known.

Ignorance does not exist.

Now I come to tell you again that this is what is true: Love is unconditional. Life is unending. God is without need. And you are a miracle. The miracle of God, made human.

This is what you have wanted to know all along. It is what you have always known in your heart, and what your mind has denied. It is what your soul has whispered time and time again, only to be silenced by your body, and the bodies around you.

You have been asked to deny Me by the very religions that would invite you to know Me. For they have told you that you are *not* Me, and I am *not* you, and that to even think so is a sin.

We are *not* one, they say, but rather, the Creator and the

created. Yet this refusal to accept and know yourself as one with Me is what has caused all of the pain and all of the sorrow of your life.

I invite you now to a meeting with the Creator.

You will find the Creator within.

15.

Using the Illusions

In preparation for your meeting with the Creator, it will serve you well to step away from your illusions—including the Illusion that you and the Creator are separate.

That is what you are doing here. That has been the purpose of this entire conversation with God. For you seek now to live *with* the Illusions, and not *within* them. And it is that honest seeking which has brought you here, to this communication.

It has been clear to you for some time that there is a flaw in the Illusions. This should have revealed all of them as false, but humans knew at some very deep level that they could not *give up* the Illusions, or something very vital would come to an end.

And, they were right. But they made a mistake. Instead of seeing the Illusions *as* illusions, and using them for the purpose for which they were intended, they thought they had to *fix the flaw.*

The answer was never to fix the flaw but merely to see it,

and thus to remember what you knew at a very deep level. And that is why you could not give up the Illusions without something very vital coming to an end.

This has been explained to you before in our conversation. I will explain it to you again, here, one final time, so that you may be absolutely clear in your remembering.

The reason for the Illusions is to provide a localized context field within which you may re-create yourself anew in the next grandest version of the greatest vision you ever held about Who You Are.

The Universe itself is a contextual field. That is both its definition and its *purpose.* It provides life with a way to be expressed and experienced physically.

You are a localized version of that same contextual field, as is everyone and everything else around you. In other words, *localized God.*

Outside of this localized context, you can only know yourself as All That Is. And All That Is cannot experience Itself as what it is, since there is nothing else.

In the absence of that which you are not, That Which You *Are* is not. It cannot be experienced. It cannot be known.

This you have been told many times.

You have been told that in the absence of fast, "slow" is not. In the absence of up, "down" is not. In the absence of here, "there" is not.

In the absence of the Illusions, then, you are—quite literally—*neither here nor there.*

And so, you have collectively produced these magnificent Illusions. A world—and indeed, a Universe—of your own creation. This has provided you with a contextual field within which you may decide and declare, create and express, experience and fulfill Who You Really Are.

You have all done this. The lot of you. Every one of you who are the individuations of the Divine Whole. You are, each of you, seeking to know yourself, to define yourself.

Who are you? Are you good? Are you bad? What _is_ "good"? What _is_ "bad"? Are you big? Are you small? What is "big"? What is "small"? Are you any of these things? What does it mean to be these things? Are you wondrous indeed?

This is the only question God ever had.

Who am I? Who am I? _Who am I?_

And who do I now choose to be?

This is the only question that matters, and this is what your soul is using your life to decide, every moment.

Not to find out. To _decide._ For life is not a process of discovery, _it is a process of creation._

Every act is an act of self-definition.

God is in the process of self-creation and self-experience in every moment. _That is what you are doing here._ And you are using the experience of that which you are not in order to have the experience of That Which You Really Are.

There _is_ nothing which you are not. You are all of it, you are everything. God is All Of It. God is everything. Yet for you (God) to know the part of it that you are now expressing, you must imagine that there are parts of it that you are not. This is the Great Imagining. These are the Illusions of Life.

Therefore, use the Illusions, and be grateful for them. Your life is a magic trick, and you are the magician.

Expressing the glory of Who You Are in the moment that you are confronted with an Illusion is what the journey to mastery is about. Within this context, it is important to acknowledge that the Illusions can seem very real.

Understanding that the Illusions *are* illusions is the first step in using them for their intended purpose, but it is not the only step. Next comes your decision about what the Illusions mean.

Finally, you choose the aspect of Divinity (the part of your self) that you wish to experience within a localized contextual field (what you would call a "situation" or "circumstance") that you have encountered (created).

Here is that process in brief:

A. See the Illusions *as* Illusions.
B. Decide what they mean.
C. Re-create yourself anew.

There are many ways to use The Ten Illusions, and many ways to experience them. You may choose to experience them as present-moment realities, or as memories from the past. The latter is how the Illusions are used by advanced cultures and beings.

Highly evolved beings remain aware of the Illusions, and they never end them (remember, to end them would be to end life itself, as you know it), but they experience them as part of their past, rather than part of their present. They encourage each other to always remember them but never to live them as if they were here-and-now realities ever again.

Yet, whether you experience them in present time or as reminders from the past, the important thing is to see them for

what they are—Illusions. Then you can use them for what
you will.

If it is your will to experience a particular aspect of you,
the Illusions are your tools. Each Illusion may be used to experience many aspects of Who You Are, and you may com-
bine Illusions to experience multiple aspects—or to
experience an individual aspect in multiple ways.

For instance, the First and Fourth Illusion—Need and Insufficiency—may be combined to experience a particular nuance of your true being that you might call self-assurance.

You cannot feel self-assured if there is nothing to feel self-
assured about. By using the Illusion of Need and Insufficiency,
you can first entertain the idea that there is "not enough," and
then overcome it. By doing this repeatedly, you produce the
experience of self-assurance, confident that there will always
be enough of whatever you need. This experience will be ver-
ified and validated by Ultimate Reality.

This is what is meant when it is said that one is "entertaining an idea." You are in the process of re-creating yourself
anew—and this is *true recreation!*

To use another in an infinite number of examples, the Second and Sixth Illusion—Failure and Judgment—may be combined for a particular effect or experience. You can allow
yourself to imagine that you have failed, then you can judge
yourself for it, or accept the judgment of others. Then you
can rise above your "failure," raising your fist to the sky with
an "I'll show you" attitude, and triumph in the end!

This is a delicious experience, and most of you have given
this experience to yourself many times. Yet if you lose sight of

the fact that Failure and Judgment are Illusions, you could find yourself stuck in those experiences, and they will soon seem like harsh realities indeed.

The movement away from the "harsh realities" of life is to step away from the Illusions, and to see them for what they really are.

Any of the Illusions may be combined with any other—Disunity with Need, Condemnation with Superiority, Ignorance with Superiority, Insufficiency *and* Condemnation with Failure, and so on. Standing alone or combined with others, the Illusions exist as magnificent *contrasting contextual fields,* allowing you to experience Who You Really Are.

It has been said to you many times that, in the relative world, you cannot experience Who You Are except in the space of that which you are not. The purpose of the Illusions is to provide precisely that—a space, a context, within which to experience every aspect of yourself, and an opportunity to choose the Highest Aspect of which you can then conceive, in any given moment.

Do you understand now? Do you see?

Good. Let's look at the Illusions one by one now, with some examples of how they may be utilized to re-create yourself anew in the way that has been described here.

The First Illusion, the Illusion of Need, may be used to experience the huge aspect of Who You Are that you might conceptualize as: that which needs nothing.

You need nothing to exist, and you need nothing to continue existing forever. The Illusion of Need creates a contextual field within which you can have the experience of that. It is when you step outside of the Illusion that you experience Ultimate Reality. The Illusion creates a context within which Ultimate Reality may be understood.

The Ultimate Reality is that everything you think you need, you already have. It exists inside of you. Indeed, it *is* you. You *are* what you need—and, therefore, you give yourself everything you need in any given moment. This means, in effect, that you need nothing at all. To understand this, and to know it experientially, you must see the Illusion of Need as an illusion. You must step outside of it.

The way to step outside of the Illusion of Need is to look at what you think you need right now—that is, what you think you do not now have that you feel you must have—and then notice that, even though you are without it, *you are still here.*

The implications of this are enormous. If you are here, right now, without what you think you need, *then why do you think you need it?*

That is the key question. It will unlock the golden door, the door to everything.

The next time you imagine that you need something, ask yourself: "Why do I think I need this?"

This is a very liberating inquiry. It is freedom in seven words.

If you are seeing clearly, you will realize that you do *not* need whatever "it" is, that you never did need it, and that *you have been making it all up.*

Even the air you breathe, you do not need. You will notice this the moment you die. Air is something that only your body needs, and you are not your body.

Your body is something that you have, it is not something that you are. It is a wonderful tool. Yet you do not need your present body to continue the process of creation.

This information may be esoterically pleasing but may do nothing to alleviate your fear of losing your body, your family, and the circumstance in which you find yourself. A way to alleviate such fears is through detachment—the practice of Masters. Masters have learned to achieve detachment before they have evidence that the life of the body is an illusion. For those not operating at the level of mastery, the experience of what you call death is often needed to provide this evidence.

Once you are away from your body (that is, once you have "died"), you will realize immediately that this state of being is not the dreaded experience of which you have heard, and is, in fact, an experience of glorious wonder. You will see, too, that it is infinitely preferable to being tied to your physical form, *whatever* attachments your most recent form may have created. Detachment will then be a simple matter.

Yet you can master Life while *in* your physical form, and do not have to wait until you are removed from it to know the glory of life, and of Who You Are. You can do this by achieving detachment *before* you die. And you can achieve *this* through the simple expediency of stepping away from the Illusion of Need.

This stepping away is accomplished through a deeper comprehension of both life and death, including the knowledge that death as you have conceived of it does not exist, and that Life goes on forever. When you understand this, it becomes possible to detach from anything in Life—including

Life Itself—because you know, given that life goes on forever, that *you may have those attachments again, as well as others that you might have thought you would nevermore experience.*

All of your earthly attachments, in fact, may be experienced in what you call the "afterlife," *or in any future life,* and so, you will have the experience that you have lost nothing at all. Gradually, you will release yourself from your attachments, as you become aware of the extraordinary opportunities for continued expansion and growth that never-ending Life offers you.

Yet you will never stop loving those you have loved, in this or any other lifetime, and you will experience full Oneness with them at the level of Essence at any time that you wish.

Should you miss someone who is still living with a physical body on Earth, you can be with them with the speed of your thought.

Should you miss someone who has already left the body, a loved one who has died before you, you will be reunited following your own death, if that is what you choose, or at any moment that you wish—again, with the speed of your thought.

This is only part of the wonder of what is to come. I will tell you more—much more—in a future communication focusing on the experience of dying with God.

You cannot die without God, but you can imagine that you are doing so. This is your imaginary hell, the fear of which has sponsored every other fear you have ever had. Yet you have nothing to fear, and there is nothing you need, for not only is it impossible for you to die without God, it is also impossible for you to live without God.

This is because I am you, and you are Me, and there is no separation between us. You cannot die without Me, because "without Me" is not a state in which you can, or will ever, find yourself.

I am God, and I am All That Is. Since you are a part of All That Is, *I am what you are.* There is not a part of you that I am not.

And if All That Is is always with you, then you need nothing—and that is the truth of your being. When you deeply understand this, you will live in your body in an entirely different way. You will become fearless—and fearlessness produces its own blessing, for lack of fear creates a lack of anything to be afraid of.

Conversely, the presence of fear draws to you that which you fear. Fear is a strong emotion, and strong emotion—energy in motion—is creative. This is why I have inspired it to be said, "You have nothing to fear, but fear itself."

The way to live without fear is to know that every outcome in life is perfect—including the outcome that you fear most, which is death.

I am telling you that here. I am giving you this information now. If you will look closely at your life, you will see that you have always had whatever you have needed in order to get to the next moment, and, ultimately, to bring you here, where you are, right now. The evidence of this is the fact that you *are* here. Clearly, you have needed nothing more. You may have wanted something more, but you have *needed* nothing more. *All your needs have been met.*

This is an amazing revelation, and it is always true. Every appearance to the contrary is False Evidence Appearing Real (FEAR). Yet, "Fear not, for I am with you."

When you know that everything turns out perfectly and there is nothing of which to be afraid, conditions that you would once have defined as fearful are seen in an entirely different light. Indeed, they are seen *in* the light, rather than in the darkness, and you begin to call your fears "adventure."

Such a recontextualization can change your life. You can live without fear, and you can experience the glory for which you were created. Seeing the Illusion of Need as an illusion allows you to use the Illusion for the purpose for which it was intended—as a tool with which you can experience this glory, and know yourself as Who You Really Are.

Using the illusion that you need your body, for instance, motivates you to protect it, to care for it, to make sure it is not abused. In this way, the body may be used for the greater glory for which it was intended.

Using the illusion that you need a relationship likewise motivates you to protect that relationship, to care for it, to make sure it is not abused. In this way, the relationship may be used for the greater glory for which it was intended.

The same is true of anything that you imagine that you need. *Use* the imagining. Use it in very practical ways. Yet know that it only serves you when you see that it is an Illusion. As soon as you believe that the Illusion is real, then you turn caution (a very purposeful use of an Illusion) into fear, and begin to cling. Love becomes possession, and possession becomes obsession. You have fallen into the trap of attachment. You have become lost in the Illusion.

And when you are lost in the Illusion of Need, you are lost indeed. For the Illusion of Need is the biggest Illusion of all. It is The First Illusion, and the most powerful. It is the Illusion upon which all other Illusions are based. Who You Are is that which is *without* need, and it is *Who You Are* that is *lost.*

It is often said of a person that "he is just trying to find himself." And that is *very true.* What you are all trying to find is your self. Yet you will not find that self anywhere outside of you. What you are looking for can only be found within.

Remember what I have told you: If you do not go within, you go without.

Only within can you find your answer to the question, "Why do I think I need this external person, place, or thing?" Only within can you remember that you do not. Then you will know what is meant by, *"Once I was lost, but now I am found."*

What you will have found is your true identity. You have used The First Illusion to experience yourself as a Divine being who needs nothing, for every need is always met. As you awaken to this truth, you will experience it more and more in your day-to-day reality. And you will literally become what you know yourself to be.

Always remember that.

You become what you know yourself to be.

The Second Illusion, the Illusion of Failure, may be used to experience your inability to fail at anything.

Nothing you do is a failure but merely part of the process

you have undergone to achieve what you are seeking to achieve, and to experience what you are seeking to experience.

What you are seeking to experience is That Which You Are. You cannot experience That Which You Are in the absence of that which you are not. Therefore, know that when you experience that which you are not, it is not a *failure* to experience but a *way* to experience That Which You Are.

What was just said is very important, yet it is easy to move right through statements like that and miss their enormous significance. So I am going to repeat the statement.

When you experience that which you are not, it is not a *failure* to experience but a *way* to experience That Which You Are.

And so, when what you call "failure" visits your life, embrace it lovingly, do not condemn it and make it wrong. For what you resist persists, and what you look at disappears. That is, it ceases to have its illusory form. You see it for what it really is, just as you see yourself as Who You Really Are.

By using the Illusion of Failure to notice what you have learned (remembered) about life, and to motivate you to apply the wisdom that you have acquired, the Illusion becomes a tool with which to notice that you are always succeeding.

Put simply, the way to step outside of the Illusion of Failure is to simply see everything as a part of your success. All things lead to your success, produce your success, are part of the process by which you experience your success.

Many people understand this intuitively. Scientists are among them. When they embark on an important experiment, they not only anticipate failure, *they relish it*. The pure scientist understands completely that a "failed" experiment has not "failed" at all but merely pointed the way to success.

Something working out "the way you wanted it to" is not the definition of success, and something "not working out the way you wanted it to" is not the definition of failure. Indeed, if you live a long life there will be times when you will claim the opposite to be true.

What you call many failures are actually successive experiences. And how can any experience which you call "successive" be a _failure?_

Yet the _Illusion_ of Failure is necessary in order to experience the exhilaration of success. If you "succeed" at everything, then you will experience succeeding at nothing. You will simply feel that you are doing what you are doing, but you will not know it as success, nor experience the wonder and the glory of Who You Are, because there would be no contextual field within which to notice that.

If you throw a touchdown pass on the first attempt, that may be exhilarating, for sure. Yet if you throw a touchdown pass on _every_ attempt, you would soon lose the excitement of it. It would mean nothing. There would be nothing _but_ touchdown passes, and throwing them would be pointless, meaningless.

All of life moves in cycles. And it is these cycles that give meaning to life.

In fact, _there is no such thing as failure._ There is only success, manifesting in its many aspects. There is also no such thing as that which is not God. There is only God, manifesting in Its many aspects.

Do you see the parallel? Do you see the model?

This simple seeing changes everything. When this is clear to you, you will be immediately struck with gratitude and wonder. Gratitude for all of the "failures" of your life, and wonder that it took so long to recognize the treasures that you have been given.

You will understand at last that truly "I have brought you nothing but angels," and "I have given you nothing but miracles."

In the moment of this understanding, you will know that you never fail to succeed.

Always remember that.

You never fail to succeed

The Third Illusion, the Illusion of Disunity, may be used to experience your unity with everything.

If you are united with something for a long time, you will at some point cease to notice that there is a "you" at all. The idea of "you" as a separate entity will gradually disappear.

People who have been together for a very long time often experience this. They begin to lose their individual identity. This is one-derful—to a point. Yet the wonder of it disappears when the Unity is experienced without end, because Unity in the absence of Disunity is nothing. It is not experienced as ecstasy but as a void. In the absence of any separation, *ever,* Oneness is noneness.

That is why I have inspired it to be written: Let there be spaces in your togetherness. Drink from a full cup but not from the same cup. The pillars that support a structure stand apart, and the strings of the lute are separate, though they quiver with the same music.

All of life is a process of experiencing Unity and separation, Unity and separation. This is the very rhythm of life. Indeed, this is the rhythm that creates Life Itself.

I say to you again: Life is a cycle, as is everything in it. The cycle is to and fro, to and fro. Together, apart. Together, apart.

Even when a thing is apart, it is always together, for it cannot truly separate, but only get larger. Therefore, even when a thing appears to be apart, it is still a part, which means it is not apart at all.

Your entire Universe was once unified beyond comprehension, compacted into a dot infinitesimally smaller than the period at the end of this sentence. It then exploded, yet it did not truly separate but merely became larger.

God cannot dismember Itself. We can *appear* to have come apart, but we have all simply become *a part.* Our intrinsic Unity is experienced once again when we re-member.

When you see others who appear separate from you, look at them deeply. Look *into* them. Do this for a long moment and you will capture their essence.

And then you'll meet you, waiting there.

When you see things in your world—a part of nature, another aspect of life—that appear separate from you, just look at them deeply. Look *into* them. Do this for a long moment and you will capture their essence.

And then you'll meet you, waiting there.

In that moment you will know Unity with all things. And

as your sense of Oneness increases, suffering and sorrow will vanish from your life, for suffering is a response to separation, and sorrow is an announcement of its truth. Yet it is a false truth. It is something that only appears to be true. It is not ultimately true. True separation, from anyone or anything, is simply not possible. It is an illusion. It is a wonderful illusion, because it allows you to experience the ecstasy of Union, but it is an illusion nonetheless.

Use the Illusion of Disunity as if it were a tool in the hands of a craftsman. Craft your experience of total unification with this tool, and use the tool again to re-create the experience over and over again.

When you see nothing but you wherever you look, you peer through the eyes of God. And as your sense of Oneness increases, pain and disappointment will vanish from your life.

Always remember that.

As your sense of Oneness increases, pain and disappointment will vanish from your life.

The Fourth Illusion, the Illusion of Insufficiency, may be used to experience your abundance.

God is abundant, and so are you. In the Garden of Eden you had everything, but you did not know it. You experienced eternal life, but it did not matter. It did not impress you because you experienced nothing else.

The Garden of Eden is a myth, but the story was intended to convey a great truth. When you have everything and do not know that you have everything, you have nothing.

The only way for you to know what it means to have everything is for you to at some point have less than everything. Hence, the Illusion of Insufficiency.

Your insufficiency was intended as a blessing, through which you could know and experience your true and total abundance. Yet it is necessary to step outside of the Illusion—to see the Illusion *as* an illusion, and move away from it—in order to have this experience.

Here's how you can step outside of the Illusion of Insufficiency: Fill the insufficiency that you see, wherever you see it outside of yourself. For this is where the Illusion lies: outside of yourself. If, then, you see insufficiency outside of yourself, *fill the insufficiency.*

If you see people who are hungry, feed them. If you see people who need clothing, clothe them. If you see people who need shelter, give them shelter. You will then experience that you have no insufficiencies at all.

However little of anything you have, you can always find someone who has less. Find that someone, and give to them from the abundance that is yours.

Seek not to be the recipient of anything but to be the source. That which you wish to have, cause another to have. That which you would seek to experience, cause another to experience. In so doing, you will remember that you have had these things in your possession all along.

This is why it has been said, "Do unto others as you would have them do unto you."

So don't go around asking, What are we to eat? What are we to drink? Look at the birds in the air. They neither sow, nor do they reap, nor gather into barns, and yet they are fed.

Which of you, by being anxious, can add one thing to your life?

And do not ask, How shall we clothe ourselves? Consider the lilies of the field, and how they grow. They neither toil, nor do they spin. Yet I tell you, even Solomon in all his glory was not arrayed like one of these.

Therefore, seek ye first the kingdom of heaven, and all else will be added unto you.

And how may you seek the kingdom of heaven? By providing the kingdom of heaven to others. By _being_ the kingdom of heaven, in which others may find refuge and strength. By _bringing_ the kingdom of heaven, and all its blessings, to all those whose lives you touch. For what you give, you become.

Always remember that.

What you give, you become.

The Fifth Illusion, the Illusion of Requirement, may be used to experience that there is nothing you have to do to know and experience Who You Really Are.

Only by doing those things that you imagine you are required to do to make life work can you come to a complete knowing that none of it is necessary.

Ask those among you who are very old. Ask those who have danced the dance and toed the line and obeyed the rules. They will give you their advice in three words.

"Disobey the rules."

They will not hesitate. Their counsel will be quick and clear.

"Color outside the lines."

"Don't be afraid."

"Listen to your heart."

"Don't let *anyone* tell you what to do."

At the end of your life you will know that nothing you have done will matter—*only who you have been while you have done it.*

Have you been happy? Have you been kind? Have you been gracious? Have you been caring, and compassionate, and considerate of others? Have you been generous, and sharing, and—most of all—have you been loving?

You will see that it is who you have *been,* not what you have *done,* that matters to your soul. And you will see that it is your soul, after all, that is Who You Are.

Yet the Illusion of Requirement, the idea that there are things you must do, can serve to motivate your mind while you are with your body. It is useful as long as you understand at some level that it is an Illusion, and that *nobody has to do anything that they don't want to do.*

For most people this truth is both incredibly freeing and incredibly frightening. The fear is that if human beings were really allowed to do only what they wanted to do, nothing that truly needs to be done would ever get done.

Who would take the garbage out?

Seriously.

Who would do the things that nobody wants to do?

That is the question, that is the fear. Humans believe that, left to their own devices, people would not do what needs to be done to keep life going.

That fear is unfounded. Humans, it would be discovered, are pretty wonderful beings. And in a community where there were no rules, no regulations, and no requirements, there would still be plenty of people who would do the things that need to be done. In fact, there would be very few who would not, for they would be uncomfortable being known as non-contributors.

And that is what would change if there were no rules, regulations, or requirements. What would change is not what is being done, but *why* it is being done.

The "why" of doing would be altered.

Instead of doing things because they are told they must, humans would do what they do because they *choose to,* as an expression of Who They Are.

This is, in truth, the only real reason to do anything. But it reverses the entire doing-being paradigm. The way humans have constructed the paradigm, one does something, and then one is something. Under the new paradigm, one is something, and then one does something.

One *is* happy, and then one does what a happy person does. One *is* responsible, and then one does what a responsible person does. One *is* kind, and then one does what a kind person does.

One does not do responsible things in order to be responsible. One does not do kind things in order to be kind. This only leads to resentment ("After all I've done!"), because it assumes that all the doing will be rewarded.

And that is precisely what you have deemed the purpose of heaven.

Heaven has been held out as your eternal reward for all the things you have done while on Earth—and for not doing the things you were "not supposed to do." So you have decided that there must also be a place for people who have not done good things, or who have done things they were not supposed to do. You have called this place hell.

Now I come to tell you this: There is no such place as hell. Hell is a state of being. It is the experience of separation from God, an imagining that you are separate from your very self and cannot be reunited. Hell is forever trying to find your self.

What you have called heaven, too, is a state of being. It is the experience of Oneness, the ecstasy of reunification with All That Is. It is the knowing of the true self.

There are no requirements for heaven. That is because heaven is not a place that you *get* to, it is a place that you are *in, always.* Yet you can be in heaven (Oneness with All) and not know it. Indeed, most of you are.

This can be changed, but not by something you are doing. It can only be changed by something that you are *being.*

This is what is meant by, "There is nothing you have to do." There is nothing to do but be.

And there is nothing to be but One.

The amazing thing is that when you are being One with everything, you wind up doing *all the things you thought you "had to do"* in order to receive the reward you thought you had to work so hard to receive. It becomes your natural will to do to, and for, others only those things that you would do to and for yourself. And you would not do to others what you would not want done to you. When you are being One, you are realizing—that is, *making real*—the idea that there is no "other."

Yet even being One is not "required." You cannot be required to be what you already are. If you have blue eyes, no-body can make you have blue eyes. If you are six feet tall, no one can force you to be six feet tall. And if you are One with everything, you cannot be *required to be.*

Therefore, there is no such thing as Requirement.

Requirement does not exist.

Who would do the requiring? And of whom would it be required? *There is only God.*

I Am That I Am, and there is nothing else that is.

Use the Illusion of Requirement to notice that there can be nothing that is truly required. You cannot know and experience freedom from Requirement if you have nothing *but* freedom from Requirement. You will seek to imagine, therefore, that certain things are required of you.

This you have done very well. You have created a God who demands perfection of you, and who requires you to come to Him in only a certain way, through particular rituals, all of which are carefully prescribed. You must say the exact and perfect words, do the exact and perfect things. You must live in a particular way.

Having created the illusion that such requirements exist in order to acquire My love, you are now beginning to experience the indescribable joy of knowing that none of this is necessary.

You will notice this by observing that "rewards" often come to people on Earth whether they "do what they are supposed to do" or not. The same is true of what you imagine your rewards to be in your afterlife. Yet your experience in the afterlife is not a reward, it is an outcome. It is the natural result of a natural process called Life.

When you become clear about this, you will understand free will at last.

In that moment, you will know that your true nature is freedom. You will never again confuse love with Requirement, for true love requires nothing.

Always remember that.

True love requires nothing.

The Sixth Illusion, the Illusion of Judgment, may be used to experience the wonder of a non-judgmental you, and a non-judgmental God.

You have chosen to create the experience of judgment in order to experience the wonder of a non-judgmental God, and to understand that judgment is utterly impossible in God's world. Only through feeling the sadness and the destructiveness of judgment yourself could you truly know that it is not something that love could ever sponsor.

It is when other people judge you that you know this most keenly, for nothing hurts more than judgment.

Judgment hurts deeply when those who judge you are wrong—yet it hurts even more deeply when they are right. This is when the judgment of others cuts to the quick, tearing at the fabric of the soul. You have only to experience this once to know that judgment is never a product of love.

In creating your illusory world, you have produced societies in which judgment is not only accepted but expected. You have even created an entire system of what you call "justice" around this idea that someone else can judge you to be "guilty" or "innocent."

I tell you this: No one is ever guilty, and everyone is forever innocent, in the eyes of God. That is because My eyes see more than yours. My eyes see why you think things, why you say things, and why you do things. My heart knows that you have merely misunderstood.

I have inspired it to be said, "No one does anything inappropriate, given their model of the world." This is a great truth. I have inspired it to be said, "Guilt and fear are the only enemies of man." That is a great truth.

In highly evolved societies, no members of those societies are ever judged and found guilty of anything. They are simply observed to have done something, and the outcome of their actions, the impact of them, is made clear to them. Then they are allowed to decide what, if anything, they wish to do with regard to that. And others in the society are likewise allowed to decide what, if anything, they wish to do to and for themselves with regard to that. They do nothing to another. The idea of punishment is simply not something that occurs to them, because the concept of punishment itself is incomprehensible to them. Why would the One Being want to hurt Itself? Even if It has done something that is damaging, why would It want to hurt Itself again? How does hurting Itself once more correct the damage of the first hurt? It's like stubbing one's toe, then kicking twice as hard to retaliate.

Of course, in a society that does not see itself as one, and does not see itself as one with God, this analogy would not make sense. In such a society, judgment would make perfect sense.

Judgment is not the same as observation. An observation is a simple looking, a simple seeing of what is so. Judgment, on the other hand, is a concluding that something *else* must be so because of what is observed.

Observing is witnessing. Judging is concluding. It is adding a "therefore" to the sentence. In fact, it *becomes* a sentence—often handed down without mercy.

Judgment sears the soul, for it brands the spirit with an Illusion of who you are, ignoring the deeper reality.

I will never judge you, ever. Because even if you have done a certain thing, My observation of that would be a simple seeing of what is so. I would draw no conclusions about Who You Are. It is, in fact, impossible to draw conclusions about Who You Are, because in your creation of yourself you are never concluded. You are a work in progress. You are not finished creating you—*and you never will be.*

You are never who you were in the last moment. And I never see you as that, but, rather, as who you *now* choose to be.

I have inspired others to describe it this way: You are continually creating yourself from the field of infinite possibilities. You are constantly re-creating your self anew in the next grandest version of the greatest vision you ever held about Who You Are. You are, in every moment, born again. And so is everyone else.

In the moment you understand this you will see that judging yourself, or judging another, is pointless. Because that which you would judge *has ceased to be,* even as you are judging it. It has come to a conclusion even as you are coming to your own conclusions.

In that moment you will relinquish forever your idea of a judging God, for you will know that love could never judge.

As your awareness increases, you will comprehend the full impact of the truth that self-creation never ends.

Always remember that.

Self-creation never ends.

The Seventh Illusion, the Illusion of Condemnation, may be used to experience the fact that you are deserving of nothing but praise. This is something that you cannot fathom, for you live so deeply within your Illusion of Condemnation. If, however, you lived within the heart of praise every moment, you could not experience it. Praise would mean nothing to you. You would not know what it was.

The glory of praise is lost when praise is all there is. Yet you have taken this awareness to an extreme, taking the illusion of imperfection and Condemnation to new levels, where you now actually believe praise to be wrong—especially self-praise. You are not to praise yourself, or to notice (much less announce) the glory of Who You Are. And you must be sparing in your praise of others. Praise, you have concluded, is not good.

The Illusion of Condemnation is also your announcement that you, and God, can be damaged. Exactly the opposite is true, of course, but you cannot know this truth, nor experience it, in the absence of any other reality. And so, you have created an alternate reality in which damage is possible, and Condemnation is proof of it.

To repeat, the idea that you, or God, can be damaged is an illusion. If God is the All In All (and I am), and if God is the Most Powerful (and I am), and if God is the Supreme Being (it is true), then God is incapable of being hurt or damaged. And if you are made in the image and likeness of God (and you are), then you cannot be hurt or damaged either.

Condemnation is a device you have created to help you experience the wonder of this, by producing a context within which this truth can have meaning. "Damage" is one of the many lesser illusions that evolve every day from The Ten Illusions. The First Illusion (that God and you need something) is what creates the illusion—that if you don't get what you need, God and you will be injured, hurt, or damaged.

This sets up the perfect case for *retribution.* And this is not a small but a very big illusion.

Nothing has captured the imagination of humans more completely than the idea that hell exists, that there is a place in the Universe to which God condemns those who have not obeyed His law.

Frightening, gruesome pictures of this horrific place appear in frescoes on the ceilings and walls of churches all over the world. Equally upsetting images adorn the pages of catechism texts and Sunday-school booklets given to little children—the better to scare them with.

And while good, church-going people have for centuries believed the message that these images send, it happens that the message is false. That is why I inspired Pope John Paul II to indicate to a Papal Audience at the Vatican (July 28, 1999) that "improper use of biblical pictures must not create psychosis or anxiety." The biblical descriptions of hell are symbolic and metaphorical.

I inspired the Pope to say that the "inextinguishable fire"

and "the burning oven" the Bible speaks of "indicate the complete frustration and vacuity of a life without God." Hell is a state of separation from God, he explained, a state caused not by a punishing God but rather, *self-induced.*

It is not God's function to administer retribution or to punish anyone, and the Pope made that clear in his Audience.

Still, the idea of a condemning God has been a useful illusion. It has created a context within which you could experience all manner of things, many aspects of being.

Fear, for instance. Or forgiveness. Compassion, and mercy, too.

A condemned man understands, at the deepest level, the expression of mercy. So does the person doing the condemning—or the granting of pardon.

Forgiveness is another nuance of the expression of love that it has served your species to experience. Forgiveness is experienced only in young, primitive cultures (advanced cultures have no need for it, understanding that, since there can be no damage, no forgiveness is necessary), but it has enormous value within the context of evolution—the process by which cultures mature and grow.

Forgiveness allows you to heal virtually any psychological, emotional, spiritual, and sometimes even physical, wound that you imagine has been inflicted upon you. Forgiveness is a great healer. You can literally forgive your way to health. You can forgive your way to happiness.

Your use of the Illusion of Condemnation has been very creative in this regard, creating many moments in your life, and in human history, in which forgiveness could be expressed. You have experienced this as an aspect of divine love—moving you closer and closer to the truth of both love and Divinity itself.

One of the most famous stories of forgiveness that has done this is the account of Jesus forgiving the man on the cross beside Him, revealing the eternal truth that *no one is condemned who seeks God.* This means that no one is ever condemned, because everyone ultimately seeks God, whether they call it that or not.

Hell is the experience of separation from God. Yet anyone who does not wish to experience eternal separation *does not have to.* The mere desire for reunion with God produces it.

That is an extraordinary statement, and I am going to repeat it.

The mere desire for reunion with God produces it.

Forgiveness is never necessary, since no true offense can ever be committed by or against Divinity itself, given that Divinity itself is All That Is. This is something that advanced cultures understand. Who would forgive whom? And, for what?

Does the hand forgive the toe for stubbing itself? Does the eye forgive the ear?

The hand may comfort the toe, true enough. It may rub it and heal it and make it better. But does it need to *forgive* the toe? Or could it be that *forgiving* is just another word for *comforting* in the language of the soul?

I have inspired it to be written: *Love means never having to say you're sorry.*

When your culture, too, understands this, you will never again condemn yourself or another for those times when the soul is "stubbing a toe." You will never again embrace a vengeful, angry, damning God who would condemn you to everlasting torture for what would, to God, surely be less than the stubbing of a toe.

In that moment, you will relinquish forever your idea of a condemning God, for you will know that love could never condemn. Then you will condemn no one and nothing, either, according to My injunction: Judge not, and neither condemn.

Always remember that.

Judge not, and neither condemn.

The Eighth Illusion, the Illusion of Conditionality, may be used to experience that aspect of your self which exists without condition—and which can love without condition for that very reason.

You are an unconditional being, yet you cannot know that you are an unconditional being because there is no condition in which you are not unconditional. You are, therefore, in no condition.

This is true, literally. You are in no condition to do anything. You can only be. Yet pure beingness does not satisfy you. For this reason, you have created the Illusion of Conditionality. This is the idea that one part of you—one part of Life, one part of God—depends upon another in order to be.

This is an outgrowth, or an enlargement, of your Illusion of Disunity, which, in turn, springs from your Illusion of Need, which is The First Illusion. There is really only One Illusion, and all other illusions are an enlargement of that, as I have said repeatedly.

It is from the Illusion of Conditionality that what you call relativity was created. Hot and cold, for instance, are really not opposites but *the very same thing in a different condition.*

Everything is the same thing. There is only one energy, and that is the energy you call Life. The word "God" may be used interchangeably here. It is the individual and specific vibration of this energy that you refer to as its condition. Under certain conditions, certain things occur and appear to be what you would call true.

For instance, up is down and down is up—under certain conditions. Your astronauts learned that in outer space, definitions of "up" and "down" disappeared. *Truth changed,* because conditions changed.

Changing conditions create changing truth.

Truth is nothing more than a word meaning "what is so right now." Yet what is so is always changing. Therefore, truth is always changing.

Your world has shown you this. Your life has demonstrated this to you.

The process of Life is, in fact, change. Reduced to one word, life is change.

God Is Life. Therefore, God Is Change.

In one word, God Is Change.

God is a process. Not a being, but a process.

And that process is called change.

Some of you might prefer the word evolution.

God is the energy that evolves . . . or, That Which Becomes.

That Which Becomes needs no special condition in order to become. Life simply becomes what It becomes, and in order for you to define it, describe it, quantify it, measure it, and try to control it, you ascribe certain conditions to it.

Yet Life has no conditions. It simply is. Life is what it is.

I AM THAT I AM.

You may now fully understand this ancient enigmatic statement for the first time.

When you know that conditions must appear to exist in order for you to experience *non-conditionality* (that is, in order for you to know God), you will bless the conditions of your life, and every condition that you have ever experienced. These conditions have allowed you to experience that you are larger than any of them. Larger than all of them combined. Your life has shown you this.

Think of this for a moment, and you will see that this is true. Imagine a condition in which you have found yourself, in which you have imagined yourself to be. Have you ever risen above that condition, to discover that you have overcome it? In truth, you did not overcome it at all. You never *were* it. You simply threw off your idea that this condition in which you found yourself was *you*. You saw yourself as bigger than that, other than that.

"I am not my condition," you may have said. "I am not my handicap, I am not my job, I am not my wealth, or lack of it, I am not this. *This is not Who I Am.*"

People who have made such declarations have produced extraordinary experiences in their lives, extraordinary outcomes. They have thus used the Illusion of Conditionality to re-create themselves anew, in the next grandest version of the greatest vision they ever held about Who They Are.

Because of this, there are those who have blessed the very

conditions of life that others have condemned. For they have embraced these conditions as a great gift, allowing them to see and declare the truth of their being.

When you bless the conditions of your life, you change them. For you are calling them something other than what they appear to be, even as you are calling yourself something other than what you appear to be.

It is at this point that you begin to consciously *create,* and not merely notice, the conditions and circumstances of your life, for you will know that you have always been, and always will be, the perceiver and the definer of every condition. What one person perceives as poverty, you may perceive as abundance. What one person defines as defeat, you may define as victory (as you will when you decide that every failure is a success).

Thus, you will experience your self as the creator of every condition—its "imaginer," if you will (but *only* if it is your will), since true Conditionality does not exist.

In that moment you will cease blaming any other person, place, or thing in your life for the life of your experience. And the whole of your experience—*past, present, and future*—will change. You will know that you have never truly been victimized, and what you know, you will grow. Ultimately, you will realize that there are no victims.

Always remember that.

There are no victims.

The Ninth Illusion, the Illusion of Superiority, may be used to experience that no thing is superior to any other thing, and that inferiority is likewise a fiction. All things are equal. Yet you cannot know that all things are equal when equality is all there is.

If everything is equal, then nothing is equal—for the very idea of "equalness" is something which cannot be experienced, inasmuch as there is only one thing, *and it is all equal to itself.*

A thing cannot be "unequal" to itself. If you take a thing and divide it into parts, the parts equal the whole. They are not less than the whole, simply because they have been taken apart.

Yet the *illusion* of inequality allows each of the parts to notice itself as *the part that it is,* rather than seeing itself as the whole. You cannot see yourselves as a part unless you see yourselves as apart. Do you understand? You cannot conceive of yourself as a part of God unless you imagine yourself to be apart *from* God.

Put another way, you cannot see Me unless you stand back and look at Me. Yet you cannot stand back and look at Me if you think that you *are* Me. So you must imagine that you are not Me, in order to experience Me.

You are equal to God, and this equality with God is something that you yearn to experience. You are not inferior to God, nor to anything at all, yet you cannot know or experience lack of inferiority in a context where nothing is superior. You have therefore created the Illusion of Superiority, that you might know that you are equal to everything—which is to say that you are superior to nothing.

Your oneness with God cannot be experienced outside of a context in which lack of oneness, or Disunity, is possible.

You must be *within* that context, or what we have here called the *illusion,* in order to know the truth that exists outside of the illusion. You must be "in this world but not of it."

Likewise, your equality with God, and with everything and everyone in life, is not "experienceable" unless and until you can understand *in*equality.

It is for this reason that you have created the Illusion of Superiority.

There is another benefit to the idea of Superiority as well. By imagining yourself as superior to the conditions and circumstances of your life, you allow yourself to experience the aspect of your being that is bigger than all of those conditions and circumstances—a point which was made earlier.

There is a wonderful part of you that you can call upon when faced with negative conditions and circumstances. Some of you call this courage. The Illusion of Superiority has thus been very useful to you as you have lived within the larger Illusion called Life In The Physical Realm, for it has given you the strength to rise above negative circumstances, and to overcome them.

When you see this Illusion *as* an illusion, you will understand that there is no part of you that is superior to All Of It, because every part of you is All Of It. You will then not *call* upon courage, you will know that you *are* courage. You will not *call* upon God, you will know that you *are* the aspect of God that you would call upon.

You are the caller and the called. The changer and the changed. The creator and the created. The beginning and the end. The alpha and the omega.

That is what you are, because that is what I Am. And you are made in the image and likeness of Me.

You *are* Me. I *am* you. I move in you, as you, and through you. In you I have My being.

In everyone, and all things.

Therefore, none of you is superior to another. Such a thing cannot be. Yet you have created the Illusion of Superiority that you might know the power of you—and, by extension, the power of everyone; the unity and the equality of you with God and all others; and the unity and equality of everyone with God and others.

Yet you must be told that this Illusion of Superiority is a very dangerous one, if human pain and suffering is something that you wish to avoid.

I have already told you that pain and suffering are avoided when you experience your Oneness with each other, and with God. It is the Illusion of Superiority that denies this unity, and creates even greater separation.

Superiority is the most seductive idea ever visited upon the experience of humans. It can feel so good—when you are the one who is imagining yourself to be superior. Yet it can feel so bad when another is claiming to be superior to you.

Be careful with this illusion, then, because it is a powerful one. It must be understood deeply, completely. The idea of Superiority can be a great gift within the world of relative experience, as I have shown you. It can, indeed, bring you the strength and the courage to see yourself and experience yourself as larger than your circumstance, greater than your oppressors, more than you, yourself, thought yourself to be. Yet it can be insidious.

Even religions, the one human institution which was supposedly created to bring you closer to God, have too often used Superiority as their chief tool. "Our religion is superior to the other religion," many institutions have declared, thus doing more to separate human beings on the path to God than to unite them.

States and nations, races and genders, political parties and economic systems have all sought to use their supposed Superiority to attract attention, respect, agreement, adherence, power, or, simply, members. What they have produced by using this tool has been anything but superior.

Yet the largest part of the human race seems blind or is strangely silent. It cannot see that its own superiority-based behaviors are actually producing inferiority in every way. Or it does see this, and simply refuses to admit it. The result is that the cycle of claiming Superiority as justification for its actions, and then suffering the inferior results of those actions, goes on and on.

There is a way to break out of this cycle.

See this Illusion *as* an illusion. Understand and know at last that We Are All One. The human race, and all of Life, is a unified field. *It is all One Thing.* There is, therefore, nothing to be superior *to,* and nothing that is superior to you.

This is the essential truth of the life experience. Is the tulip superior to the rose? Are the mountains more majestic than the sea? Which snowflake is the most magnificent? Is it possible that they are all magnificent—and that, celebrating their magnificence together, they create an awesome display? Then they melt into each other, and into the Oneness. Yet they never go away. They never disappear. They never cease to be. Simply, they *change form*. And not just once, but several times: from solid to liquid, from liquid to vapor, *from the seen to the unseen,* to rise again, and then again to return in new displays of breathtaking beauty and wonder. This is *Life, nourishing Life.*

This is you.

The metaphor is complete.

The metaphor is real.

You will make this real in your experience when you simply decide that it is true, and act that way. See the beauty and the wonder of all whose lives you touch. For you are each wondrous indeed, yet no one more wondrous than another. And you will all one day melt into the Oneness, and know then that you form together a single stream.

Such a knowing will change the entirety of your experience on earth. It will change your politics, your economics, your social interactions, the way you educate your young. It will bring you, at last, heaven on earth.

When you see that Superiority is an illusion, you will know that inferiority is an illusion as well. Then you will feel the wonder and power of *equality*—with each other, and with God. Your idea about yourself will become larger, and the reason for the Illusion of Superiority will have been realized. For the larger your idea of you, the larger will be your experience.

Always remember that.

The larger your idea of you, the larger will be your experience.

. . .

The Tenth Illusion, the Illusion of Ignorance, has produced the idea that you don't know any of this; that everything which has just been said is new to you, and that you can't comprehend it.

This illusion allows you to continue living in the Realm of Relativity. Yet you do not have to continue living as you have been living, in pain and in suffering, hurting yourselves and each other, waiting, waiting, waiting for better times yet to come—or for your eternal reward in heaven. You *can* have your heaven on Earth. You *can* live in your garden of paradise. You were never cast out. I would never do that to you.

You know this. In your heart, you already know this. Just as you know about the Oneness of humanity, and of all life. Just as you know about the equality of everything, and that love is unconditional. You know all these things and more, and you hold this knowing deeply in your soul.

Ignorance is an illusion. You use the Illusion wisely when you see it *as* an illusion—when you know that it is *not true* that you do not know. You *know . . . and you know that you know.*

This is what is said of all Masters.

They know that they know, and they use their knowing to live *with,* and not *within,* the illusory world in which they have placed themselves. This makes them appear in your world as if they are magicians, creating and using all Life's illusions easily.

"Not knowing" is a wonderful illusion, and useful. It allows you to know again, to learn again, to remember once more. It allows you to reexperience the cycle. To become a snowflake.

It is the Illusion that you do not know that allows you to know what you know. If you know everything, and know that you know it, then you can know nothing.

Look deeply into this truth, and you will understand it.

Give yourself the illusion, then, that you are ignorant of something. *Anything.* In that moment, you will have the experience of that of which you are *not* ignorant—and what you know will suddenly become apparent to you.

This is the wonder of humility. This is the power in the statement, "There is something here I do not know, the knowing of which could change everything." This single statement can heal the world.

The call to humility is a call to glory.

And in terms of your theology, there could be no greater tool for advancement. I have inspired it to be said that a little "humility theology" is what the world needs. A little less assurance that you know it all, and a little more willingness to continue the search, to acknowledge that there may be something you do *not* know—the knowing of which could change everything.

I say again, not knowing leads to knowing. Knowing it all leads to not knowing anything.

That is why the Illusion of Ignorance is so important. And so it is, too, with all the Illusions. They are the keys to your experience of Who You Really Are. They open the door from the Realm of the Relative to the Realm of the Absolute. The door to everything.

Yet, as with all Ten Illusions, when the Illusion of Ignorance runs away with you, when it becomes your total experience, your ever-present reality, then it no longer serves you. Then you are like the magician who has forgotten his own tricks. You become one who is fooled by his own illusions. Then will you need to be "saved" by another, someone who sees through the illusion, who wakes you up, and reminds you of Who you Really Are.

This soul will truly be your savior, even as you can truly be the savior of others by simply reminding them of Who They Really Are, by giving them back to themselves. "Savior" is just another word for "reminder." It is someone who re-minds you, someone who re-members you, causing you to be of a new mind, and to once again know yourself as a member of the Body of God.

Do this for others. For you are today's savior. You are My Beloved, in whom I am well pleased. You are the one I have sent to bring the others home.

Therefore, step out of the illusion, but not away from it. Live with it, but not within it. Do this and you will be in this world, but not of it. You will know your own magic, and what you know, you will grow. Ever larger will be your idea about your magic, until you one day understand that you *are* the magic.

Always remember that.

You are the magic.

When you use the Illusion of Ignorance, no longer living it but simply using it, you acknowledge and admit that there is much that you still do not know (do not remember), yet this very humility raises you beyond the humble, causing you to understand more, remember more, become more aware. Now you are among the *cognoscenti*—those who know.

You remember that you are simply using illusions to create a localized contextual field within which you can experience, and not merely conceptualize, any one of the myriad aspects of Who You Are. You begin using this contextual field consciously, like an artist using a paint brush, producing wonderful pictures and creating powerful and extraordinary moments—moments of grace—in which you may know your self experientially.

If you wish to experience your self as forgiveness, for instance, you could mix the Illusions of Judgment, Condemnation, and Superiority. Projecting those in front of you, you quite suddenly will find (create) people in your life who give you the opportunity to exhibit forgiveness. You can even add the Illusion of Failure, projecting it on yourself, to heighten the experience. Finally, you can use the Illusion of Ignorance, to pretend that you don't know you are doing all of this.

If you want to experience your self as compassion, or as generosity, you might mix the Illusions of Need and Insufficiency to create a contextual field within which to express those aspects of Divinity within you. You may then find yourself walking down the street, confronted by beggars. Strange, you may say to yourself, I have never seen beggars on this corner before. . . .

You feel compassion for them, and it touches your heart. You feel generosity stirring within you, and you reach into your pocket and give them some money.

Or perhaps a relative will call and ask for financial help.

You could choose to feel any one of many aspects of your being in that moment. But on this occasion, you choose kindness, caring, and love. You say, "Of course, how much do you need?"

But be careful, because if you are not careful, you will not understand how the beggar on the street, or how the relative on the phone, found their way to your life. You will forget that *you put them there.*

If you fall too deeply into the Illusion, you will forget that you have called every person, place, and event of your life *to you.* You will forget that they are there to create the perfect situation, the perfect opportunity, to know yourself in a particular way.

You will forget My grandest teaching: *I have sent you nothing but angels.*

You may cast My angels as villains in your story. If you are not careful, you will see your self as the victim, rather than the beneficiary, of the many moments of grace that have come into your life, not all of which will be initially welcome, but all of which will hold a gift for you.

Or you may decide to become a beneficiary in a way other than the one you had initially chosen. You may decide, for instance, that not only do you wish to experience compassion but also power and control. You may continue giving to the same beggar, going down to the same corner every day at the same time, until the two of you establish a ritual. You may continue giving to that relative, mailing a check every month, until the two of you establish a ritual.

Now you are in control. You have the power. You have disempowered *them*—literally, taken their power to re-create their lives away from them—so that you may feel glorified, gratified, and powerful. Suddenly, they cannot function without you. Neither the beggar nor the relative—both of whom existed for years on the planet without your help at all—can function without you. You have rendered them dysfunctional, and have created a dysfunctional relationship with them.

Instead of helping them out of the pit by throwing them a rope and pulling them up, you have tossed the rope into the pit and jumped in after it.

Watch carefully, then, your motivation for doing anything. Keep looking at your agenda. Monitor closely what aspect of your being you are experiencing. Is there a way to experience that without disempowering another? Is there a way to remember Who You Are without inviting someone else to forget who they are?

These are some of the ways you may use The Ten Illusions, and the countless smaller illusions beneath them. Now you see, now you understand, now you remember how the Illusions are used.

Remember what was said earlier. It is not necessary to use Illusions in the present moment in order to create a contextual field within which to experience higher aspects of your self. Advanced beings not only step outside of the Illusions but away from them. That is, they put the Illusions behind them and merely use _the memory of them_ to create that contextual field.

Whether you use them in memory form or in physical form in your present moment, you employ them every day. Yet if you are not using Illusions consciously—if you do not know that you have been *creating them,* and why you have done so—you could imagine yourself to be at the effect of your life, rather than at cause in the matter. You could think that life is happening *to* you, rather than *through* you.

This is what you may not have known, the knowing of which could change everything:

With regard to all that is happening in your life, you are at cause in the matter.

You understand this perfectly when you step outside of the Illusions. You experience this *in your body,* at the cellular level, when you experience communion with God.

It is this for which every soul yearns. It is this that is the ultimate purpose of all of life. You are on a journey to mastery, returning to Oneness, that you may know the wonder and the glory of God in your own soul, and express it through you, *as* you, in a thousand ways over a million moments in countless lifetimes that reach to eternity.

16.

Re-creating Your Reality

As you journey to eternity, as you move to mastery, you will find yourself confronted with many circumstances, situations, and developments in your life, some of which you may call unwelcome. The first thing that most people do in such moments is the last thing that you should do, which is to try to figure out what it all means.

Some people think that things happen for a reason, and so they try to discern what that reason is. Others say that certain things are "a sign." So they try to understand what the sign is telling them.

In one way or another, people try to find meaning in the events and experiences of their lives. Yet the fact is that nothing has any meaning at all. There is no intrinsic truth hidden in the encounters and experiences of life. *Who would hide it there? And why?*

If it were there for you to discover, wouldn't it be much more efficient to make it obvious? *If God had something to tell you, wouldn't it be a lot easier (to say nothing of kinder) to simply tell you, rather than make it a mystery that you had to solve?*

The fact is, there is no meaning to anything, *save the meaning you give it.*

Life is meaningless.

That is difficult for many humans to accept, yet it is My greatest gift. By rendering life meaningless, I give you the opportunity to decide what anything and everything means. Out of your decisions will you define yourself in relationship to anything and everything in life.

This is, in fact, *the means* by which you experience Who You Choose to Be.

This is the act of self-creation, of re-creating yourself anew in the grandest version of the greatest vision you ever held about Who You Are.

So when a particular thing happens to you, don't ask yourself why it is happening. *Choose* why it is happening. *Decide* why it is happening. If you can't choose or decide with intention, then make it all up. *You are anyway.* You are making up all the reasons for doing things, or for why things are happening the way they are. Yet most of the time you are doing this unconsciously. Now make up your mind (and your life) consciously!

Do not search for life's meaning, or the meaning of any particular event, occurrence, or circumstance. *Give it* its meaning. Then announce and declare, express and experience, fulfill and become Who You Choose to Be in relationship to it.

If you are a keen observer, you will notice that you keep

bringing yourself the same situation or circumstance over and over again in your life until you re-create yourself anew.

This is the journey to mastery.

The Master, and the student on the journey to mastery, *knows* that the Illusions are illusions, *decides* why they are there, and then consciously *creates* what will be experienced next within the self through the Illusions.

When facing any life experience, there is a formula, a process, through which you, too, may move toward mastery. Simply make the following statements:

1. Nothing in my world is real.
2. The meaning of everything is the meaning I give it.
3. I am who I say I am, and my experience is what I say it is.

This is how to work with the Illusions of Life. Now we shall take another look at a few "real life" examples and revisit some earlier observations, for emphasis brings greater clarity.

When faced with the Illusion of Need, it may seem to you as though your experience is very real.

Need will present itself to you in one of two disguises: your need, or the need of others.

When the Need appears to be yours, it will feel much more urgent. Fear could set in quickly, depending on the nature of the Need that you are imagining.

If you are imagining that you need oxygen, for instance, you may be confronted with immediate panic. This would follow logically from your belief that your life was at stake. Only a true Master, or someone who has had a near-death experience and is clear that death does not exist, would be likely to remain calm in such a circumstance. Others would have to train themselves to be.

But it is possible to do that.

The irony is that it is exactly such calm that would be called for. Only calm would be conducive to the thoughts and actions that could generate a peaceful outcome.

Divers understand this. That is why they learn not to panic when they feel they are running out of air, or when their oxygen is cut off. Others, too, have learned how to avoid panic under what many would call very stressful and fearful circumstances.

There are other less extreme, but also life-threatening, situations that could produce fear. News of a terminal illness, for example. Or an armed robbery. But there are those who have discovered that they could face a potentially life-ending disease, or even the possibility of violence to their person, with extraordinary equanimity. How did they do this? What is this about?

It all has to do with perspective.

And that is what we are talking about here—your perspective.

Seeing the illusion of death *as* an illusion changes everything. Knowing that it has no meaning except the meaning you give it allows you to decide what it means. Understanding that all of life is a process of re-creation creates a context within which you may experience Who You Really Are in relationship to death.

Jesus did this and astonished the world.

Others have done it as well, moving through death with a peaceful grace that astounds and inspires everyone around them.

Beneath the level of life-threatening experiences, Need has much less power as an Illusion.

Beneath the level of physical pain it has virtually no power at all.

Many humans, but not all, have a great deal of difficulty with physical pain. If someone were to say "this is an illusion" during a moment of pain, they might have something different to utter.

Indeed, for many, pain—and the possibility of it—is more fearful than death.

Yet this illusion, too, can be dealt with. Earlier in this communication I spoke of the difference between pain and suffering. Masters know this difference, as do all people who see the Illusions of Life for what they are.

The Illusion of Need would suggest that humans need to be pain-free in order not to suffer, in order to be happy. Yet pain and happiness are not mutually exclusive—as many women who have given birth can attest.

Freedom from pain is not a need, it is a preference. By moving Need to the level of preference you place yourself in a position of extraordinary power over the experience you are having.

You can even have power over pain—sufficient power to virtually ignore it, and often to actually make it *disappear.* Many people have demonstrated this.

Dealing with Illusions of Need that are beneath the level of physical pain is even easier.

You may think that you need a particular person to be happy, or a job to be successful, or some other emotional or physical gratification to be content. That is when you may wish to notice that you are here, right now, without it. *Why, then, do you think you need it?*

Close examination will reveal that you do *not* need it, not to survive, and not even to be happy.

Happiness is a decision, not an experience.

You can decide to be happy without what you thought you needed in order to be happy, *and you will be.*

That is one of the most important things you could ever come to understand. That is why I am revisiting this point.

Happiness is a decision, not an experience. You can decide to be happy without what you thought you needed in order to be happy, *and you will be.*

Your experience is the *result* of your decision, not the *cause* of it.

(The same is true, incidentally, of love. Love is not a reaction, love is a decision. When you remember this, you are approaching mastery.)

The second disguise of Need is that of the need of others. If you do not see this Illusion as an illusion, you could trap yourself into constantly trying to meet the needs of others, especially others you love—your children, spouses, or friends.

This can lead to quiet resentment, and then, boiling anger—on the part of both you _and_ the person being helped. The irony is that by continuing to meet the needs of others, including (and perhaps especially) children and life partners, you may do more to disempower them than to help them— another point that was made earlier.

When you see others in "need," allow yourself to use the Illusion to express the part of your self that you choose to experience. Perhaps you would choose what you would call compassion or generosity, kindness or your own abundance, or even all of the above—but be clear that you are never doing anything for another. Memorize this statement: _Everything I do, I do for myself._

That is another of the most important things you could ever come to understand. I will, therefore, repeat it.

Everything I do, I do for myself.

That is God's truth, as well as yours. The only difference is that God knows this.

There is no interest other than self interest. That is because the self is all there is. You are One with everything, and there is nothing that is not you. When you are clear about this, your definition of self-interest will change.

When faced with the Illusion of Failure, it may seem to you as though this experience is very real.

Failure will present itself in one of two disguises: your "failure," and the "failure" of others.

When faced with what appears to be failure, immediately make the three statements of ultimate truth:

1. Nothing in my world is real.
2. The meaning of everything is the meaning I give it.
3. I am who I say I am, and my experience is what I say it is.

This is the triune truth—or, the Holy Trinity.

Decide what your experience of failure means. Choose to call your failure a success. Then, re-create your self anew in the face of this failure. Decide Who You Are in relationship to the experience you are having. Do not ask yourself *why* you are having it. *There is no why, except the why you give it.*

So decide that "I have had this experience in order that I might move one step closer to the success I seek. This experience has been given to me as a gift. I embrace it and treasure it, and learn from it."

Remember that I have said *all learning is remembering.*

Therefore, *celebrate failure.* There are enlightened companies on your planet that actually do this. When a "mistake" is made, an "error" is discovered, or a "failure" is experienced, the boss invites everyone to cheer the event! That boss understands what I am telling you here—and his employees would walk off a plank into icy cold water for him. There is nothing they would not do, for he has created an environment of safety and a climate of success in which they can experience the grandest part of themselves, and of their creativity.

When faced with the Illusion of Disunity, it may seem to you as though this experience is very real.

Disunity will present itself to you in one of two disguises: your "disunity," and the "disunity" of others.

You may feel terribly disconnected from God. You may feel totally separate from your fellow humans. And you may feel that others are completely separate from you. This could create the smaller illusions of loneliness or depression.

When faced with what appears to be Disunity, immediately make the three statements of ultimate truth:

1. Nothing in my world is real.
2. The meaning of everything is the meaning I give it.
3. I am who I say I am, and my experience is what I say it is.

This invokes the triad process:

A. See the Illusion as an illusion.
B. Decide what it means.
C. Re-create yourself anew.

If you are feeling lonely, see your "aloneness" as an illusion. Decide that your loneliness means that you have not reached out enough to the world around you—how can anyone be lonely in a world full of lonely people? Then choose to re-create your self anew as one who touches others with love.

Do this for three days and your whole mood will change. Do this for three weeks and your loneliness of the moment will end. Do this for three months and you will never be lonely again.

And then you will understand that your loneliness was all an illusion, *totally controllable by you.*

Even people who are in jail cells or in sick beds, completely isolated from others, can change their outer experience by altering their inner reality. This can be done through communion with God, the very experience to which this book is leading you. For once you have a meeting with the Creator within, you will never again need anything outside of yourself to avoid feeling lonely.

Mystics and monks, religious communities and spiritual devotees throughout all of time have proven this. The inner ecstasy of spiritual communion and Oneness with all of creation (that means Me!) is unmatchable in the outside world.

Indeed, Disunity is an Illusion.

So, too, will you see *everything* as illusory, and as a blessed gift, allowing you to choose and experience Who You Really Are.

Let us take a few more examples, using a few more of the Illusions (any of them could be used, the formula is the same).

When faced with the Illusion of Condemnation, it may seem to you as though this experience is very real.

Condemnation will present itself to you in one of two disguises: your "condemnation," and the "condemnation" of others.

When faced with the Illusion of Superiority, it may seem to you as though this experience is very real.

Superiority will present itself to you in one of two disguises: your "superiority," and the "superiority" of others.

When faced with the Illusion of Ignorance, it may seem to you as though this experience is very real.

Ignorance will present itself to you in one of two disguises: your "ignorance," and the "ignorance" of others.

Do you see the pattern? Are you beginning to calculate, before I even tell you, some good ways in which you may use these Illusions?

Confronted with the condemnation of others, you will be tempted to condemn. Confronted with your condemnation, others will be tempted to condemn you.

Confronted with the superiority of others, you will be tempted to think of yourself as superior. Confronted with your superiority, others will be tempted to think of themselves as superior to you.

Do you see the pattern? Are you beginning to calculate, before I even tell you, some good ways in which you may use these Illusions?

Seeing the pattern is important. This is the pattern which you have overlaid upon the fabric of your own cultural story. This is what has caused you to experience your collective reality as it is on your planet.

You do not need Me to give you any more examples of how to step away from these Illusions and use them. Indeed, if I continue to give you specific examples, you will become dependent on Me. You will feel that you cannot understand or know how to re-create your self anew in the face of "real life," day-to-day experiences.

Thus, you will begin to pray. "God, help me!" you will call out, and then thank Me if things work out well, and curse Me if they do not—as if I were granting some wishes and denying others . . . or, worse yet, *granting the wishes of some people and denying the wishes of others.*

I tell you this: *It is not God's job to grant or deny wishes. On what basis would I do so? Using what criteria?*

Understand this, if you understand nothing else: God needs nothing.

If I need nothing, I therefore have no criteria by which I would decide whether *you* get to have something or not.

That decision is yours.

You can make that decision consciously or unconsciously.

You have been making it unconsciously for centuries. Indeed, for millennia. Here is how you can make it consciously.

A. See the Illusion as an illusion.
B. Decide what it means.
C. Re-create yourself anew.

Use the following statements of ultimate truth as tools in accomplishing the above.

1. Nothing in my world is real.
2. The meaning of everything is the meaning I give it.
3. I am who I say I am, and my experience is what I say it is.

The communication that I have been having with you here is your attempt to place into human words the complex concepts that you intuitively understand at a deep inner level of awareness.

These ideas have come to you, and through you before.

If you are not careful, it will look as if they came to someone else, through someone else. *This is an illusion.*

You have brought this experience to your self, through your self, repeatedly. This is your process of your remembering.

The opportunity now is to transform these words into an experience of the flesh by replacing your Illusions with a new lived reality. This is the transformation of life on your planet of which I have spoken. Thus, I have inspired it to be said, "And the Word was made flesh, and dwelt among us."

PART III

Meeting the Creator Within

17.

Taking Control of
Your Body

For the words here to be made flesh—for them to become more than mere sounds but physical reality in your physical world—you must pay attention to the part of your self that is physical in the world.

Your communion with God, your meeting with the creator within, begins with knowing your physical body, understanding your physical body, honoring your physical body, and using your physical body as a vehicle that is meant to serve you.

In order to do this, you must first understand that you are *not* your physical body. You are that which controls your body, lives with your body, and acts in the physical world *through* your body. But you are not the body itself.

If you imagine that you are your body, you will experience Life as an expression of the body. When you understand that you are your soul, then you will experience Life as an expression of the soul. When you acknowledge that your soul and God's are one, then you will experience Life as an expression of the One Spirit.

This will change everything.

To know your body, to understand your body, to experience your body in its fullest magnificence, seek to be with your body in a quality way. Love it, care for it, listen to it. It will tell you what is true.

Remember, the truth is what is so right now—and this is something every body knows. Therefore, listen to what your body is telling you. Remember *how* to listen. Look at what your body is showing you. Remember *how* to look.

Do not only observe other people's body language, observe your own.

Health is an announcement of agreement between your body, mind, and spirit. When you are not healthy, look to see which parts of you disagree. Perhaps it is time for you to rest your body, but your mind does not know how. Perhaps your mind is dwelling on negative, angry thoughts, or worries about tomorrow, and your body cannot relax.

Your body will demonstrate the truth to you. Simply watch it. Notice what it is showing you, listen to what it is saying.

Honor your body. Keep it in good shape. It is the most important physical tool that you have. It is a magnificent tool, an extraordinary instrument. You can subject it to untold abuse, and it will continue to serve you as best it can. But why reduce its effectiveness? Why abuse its systems?

Even as I have told you to meditate every day so that you may quiet your mind and experience your Oneness with Me, now I tell you to exercise each day.

Exercise is the meditation of the body.

It, too, allows you to feel Oneness with all of Life. You will never feel so alive, and so much a _part_ of Life, as when you exercise. Movement of the body will bring you a natural high.

That high feeling has been aptly named. You _are_ high when you are connected with the Creator! And you are connected with the Creator when your body is healthy and in tune with Life.

You are in a very high place!

Your body is nothing more than an energy system. The energy that is Life is coursing through your body. You can direct this energy. You can control it.

This energy is called by many names. Some call it _chi._ In some languages it is _ki._ There are other names as well. It is all the same thing.

When you remember how to feel this energy, its subtlety, its power, you can also remember how to control it, to direct it. There are Masters who can help you do this. They are from many disciplines, many cultures, and many traditions.

You may also do this on your own, with nothing more than your inner determination to help you. Yet if you seek the guidance of a Master, a teacher, or a guru, it is important to know how to recognize one.

You can know a Master by the way he or she teaches you to get in touch with God, by the way he or she shows you how to meet with the Creator.

If they shout at you, scream at you, exhort you, and entice you to find God outside of yourself—in their truth, in their book, in their way, in their place—then watch out. Take your "watch out," and remember that this time, it's an illusion.

If they quietly invite you to find God inside of you, if they tell you that you and I are One—and that you do not need their truth, their book, their way, or their place—then you have found a Master, if only because you have been led to the Master deep inside of you.

However you do it, by whatever means or program, keep your physical body in the shape that will most effectively support you, given what it is that you are trying to do.

Know that what you are seeking to do in this life is to express and experience the grandest version of the greatest vision ever you held about Who You Are. If you do not experience that at a conscious level, if that is not what you seem to yourself to be trying to do, then nothing in the communication I am sending you now will apply. Very little of it will make any sense.

If you *are* aware at a conscious level that this is what you have come to this life to do, it might seem, reading this communication, as if you are talking to yourself.

Which is exactly what you are doing.

So it will be no surprise that exercising the body is suggested. And a diet that serves your intention, as well. You will know exactly what that diet is, and even as you approach various foods, if you *listen to your body,* you will know instantly whether it serves you to ingest them.

You can come to this knowing by simply moving your hand slowly over the food. Your body will know at once all you need to know about whether that food is in harmony with your innermost intentions for the body and the soul. You will be able to pick up the vibration. You do not need to read diet books, you do not need to take courses, you do not need to seek outside counsel or advice. You simply need to listen to your own body, and then follow *its* advice.

18.

Taking Control of Your Emotions

After taking better care of your body, the next step in achieving communion with God through meeting with the creator within involves the controlling of your emotions. This is a simple matter of understanding what emotion is. Emotion is, simply, energy in motion.

You can take this energy and give it a *pro*-motion, or a *de*-motion.

When you demote this energy—that is, move it to the lowest level—you produce a negative emotion. When you promote it—that is, move it to the highest level—you produce a positive emotion.

Exhilarating exercise of your physical body is one way to promote, or raise up, your energy. You literally increase the vibration of this *ki* energy, which turns it into a positive emotion that is expressed through you.

Meditation is another way to raise the energy of Life that is always present in your body.

The *combination* of exercise and meditation is extremely

powerful. When this combination becomes part of your spiritual discipline, you create possibilities for enormous growth.

Using this combination reminds you that you can control, and therefore experience as you choose, both your body and your emotions. For many—indeed, for most—this is a startling remembrance.

Emotions are experiences that are chosen, not experiences to which you are subjected. This is not something that is widely understood.

The exterior circumstances of your physical life need not have anything to do with the interior experience of your spiritual life. It is not necessary for you to be pain-free in order to be free of suffering. It is not necessary for there to be a lack of disruption in your life for there to be peace.

Indeed, true Masters experience peace in the *face* of disruption and conflict, not because they have found a way to avoid it.

This inner peace is what all beings seek, because it is the essence of what all beings are. And you will always seek the experience of Who You Really Are.

You may achieve this inner peace in the face of any exterior condition or circumstance simply by understanding that you are not your body, and that nothing you see is real.

Remember that you are living The Ten Illusions. And then understand the truth about those Illusions—that you created them, and all the little illusions beneath them, so that you might decide and declare, express and experience, become and fulfill Who You Really Are.

I have said to you many times before, and I will say to you again: All of Life is a gift, and all is perfection—the perfect tool with which to create the perfect opportunity for the perfect expression of perfection itself, in, as, and through you.

When you understand this, you will remain in a state of continual appreciation. That is, you will be growing. Growth is the meaning of appreciation. When something appreciates, it becomes more than it was.

It is true that not only are you able to choose, and therefore control, your emotions in the face of any circumstance, you may also do so *before* you encounter a circumstance.

That is, you can decide *ahead of time* how you are going to put your energy into motion—what your emotion is going to be—in response to any anticipated situation in your life.

When you reach this level of mastery, you will also become able to make these same choices in your response to any *un*anticipated situation in life.

In this way you will have decided Who You Are in concert with the exterior illusions of your life, rather than in conflict.

I have explained in detail in this trilogy, which includes *Conversations with God* and in *Friendship with God,* as well as through many other sources at many other times, how this may be done. This is merely a reminder of what is so.

After remembering how to care for the physical body and control your emotions, you are ready to move to the next step in meeting with the Creator within.

19.

Cultivating Willingness

Now you have prepared the way, and all that is left is to move into willingness to have your meeting with the creator within, to experience communion with God.

This can be an encounter that you experience physically or mentally—or both. You may weep with joy, tremble with excitement, or rock in ecstasy. Or you may simply and quietly move one day into a gentle awareness that you now know.

You know about The Illusion, and The Reality.

You know about your self, and about God.

You understand the Oneness, and the individuation of the Oneness.

You understand it all.

This experience of knowing may remain with you, or it may come and go. Do not feel exhalted if it stays, and do not feel discouraged if it goes. Simply notice what is so, then choose what you next wish to experience.

Even Masters have been known to occasionally choose not to experience their mastery—sometimes for the joy of reawakening to it, and sometimes for the purpose of awakening others. This is why things can happen to Masters that you, in your place of judgment, do not think should or *could* be happening if they were "really Masters."

Therefore, judge not, and neither condemn. For you may meet your Master this very day—as the bag lady on the street, or the mugger in the park, and not only as the guru on the mountain top. In fact, rarely so. The Master who appears as a Master is seldom acknowledged, and more often rebuked. Yet the Master who walks among you, appearing as one of you, is often the Master who makes the most impact.

So be alert, for you do not know at what hour your Master may come. He may even come as what you choose to call a criminal, disobeying the most sacred laws and customs of your society, and be crucified because of it.

Yet in the aftermath will you seek to remember every word he ever spoke.

Should you achieve mastery, or rise to that level even part of the time, you, too, may be judged, condemned, and crucified by your society. For others may be afraid of you, because they may be worried that you know something they do not know, or because you are challenging something that they think they *do* know. And it is fear that turns observation into judgment, and judgment into anger.

It is as I have told you. Anger is fear, announced.

The anger of others will be part of their Illusion about who they are, and who you are. And so the Master in you will forgive them, understanding that they know not what they do.

This is the key to expressing and experiencing the Divinity within you: forgiveness.

You will not see that which is Divine in you unless and until you forgive that which you believe is not. And you will be unable to behold the Divinity in another unless and until you do the same.

Forgiveness is the expander of perception.

When you forgive yourself for that which you and others are not, then you will experience that which you and others truly are. In that moment you will understand that forgiveness itself is not necessary. For who would forgive whom? And for what?

We Are All One.

There is great peace in that, and great comfort. My peace I give to you. Peace be with you.

Forgiveness is just another word for *peace* in the language of the soul.

This is something that you deeply understand when you awaken from the dream of your imagined reality.

Your moment of awakening can come to you at any time, and through any person. Therefore, honor all times and all people, for the moment of your deliverance may be at hand. It will be your deliverance from The Illusions the moment when you can be with it but not within it.

There will be more than one such moment in your life. Indeed, your life has been created to bring you just such moments.

These are your moments of grace, when clarity and wisdom, love and understanding, guidance and insight are brought to you and through you.

These moments of grace change your life forever, and often, the lives of others as well.

Just such a moment of grace brought you to this book. That is why you are able to receive and deeply understand the present communication.

In one form, this is a meeting with the Creator.

It has come upon you through your willingness, through your openness, through your forgiveness, and through your love. Your love of self, your love of others, and your love of Life.

And, yes, your love of Me.

It is love of God that brings God to you. It is love of self that brings awareness of that part of self which *is* God—and therefore knows that God does not come *to* you but *through* you. For God is never apart from you but is always a part *of* you.

The Creator is *not* separate from the created. The lover is not separate from the beloved. That is not the nature of love, and that is not the nature of God.

Nor is it the nature of You. You are separate from nothing and no one, least of all God.

You have known this from the beginning. You have understood this always. Now, at last, you are giving your self permission to experience it; to have a true moment of grace; to be in communion with God.

What is it like to be in a state of such communion? If you are even at the edges of that experience now, you already know the answer. If you have made that connection only momentarily in meditation, you already know the answer. If you have experienced the incredible high of the most exhilarating physical experience, you already know the answer.

In a state of communion with God you will temporarily lose all sense of individual identity. Yet this will occur without any sense of loss, for you will know that you have simply realized your true identity. That is, you have *real-ized it*. You have, quite literally, *made it real*.

An indescribable bliss, an elegant ecstasy, will envelop you. You will feel merged with love, one with all. And you will never be satisfied with anything less.

People who have had this experience return to the world and their lives in a new way. They find themselves falling in love with everyone on sight. They experience Oneness with all others in surprising moments of Holy Communion.

A heightened awareness and deep appreciation of nature can bring them to unexpected tears of joy at the slightest provocation. And a new clarity about everything they are seeing in the world around them can render them transformed. They often begin moving more slowly, talking more softly, acting more gently.

These and other changes may last for several hours or several days, several months or several years—or for a lifetime. The length of the experience is purely the individual's choice. It will fade of its own accord if it is not renewed. Just as the brightness of a light fades the farther one moves away from it, the bliss of Oneness fades the longer one has been away.

To stay in the light, one must remain close to it. To stay in the bliss, one must do the same.

That is why you are urged, while living with your present Illusion, to do whatever else it takes—meditate, exercise, pray, read, write, listen to music, whatever you find that works—to ignite your awareness daily.

Then you will be in the holy place of the Most High. And you will feel high, and think highly of yourself, and of others, and of all of Life.

Then, too, you will create and contribute to Life as you have never contributed before.

20.

The Message
of the Creator

After one experience of meeting the Creator within, you will remember the message of the Creator, because it is the message of your own heart.

It is no different from the message that your heart sings every time you look into the eyes of another with love. It is no different from the message that your heart cries out when you see suffering anywhere.

This is the message that you bring to the world, and that you would leave with the world, when you are your true self.

It is the message that I leave you with now, so you may remember it once again and share it with all those whose lives you touch.

Be kind to each other, and good.

Be kind to yourself, and good, as well.

Understand that these two are not mutually exclusive.

Be generous with each other, and share.

Be generous with yourself, as well.

Know that only as you share with yourself can you share with another. For you cannot give to another what you do not have.

Be gentle with each other, and true.

Be gentle with yourself, and true, as well.

To thine own self be true, and it must follow as the night the day, thou canst not then be false to any man.

Remember always that betrayal of your self in order not to betray another is betrayal nonetheless. It is the highest betrayal.

Remember always that love is freedom. You need no other word to define it. You need no other thought to comprehend it. You need no other action to express it.

Your search for the true definition of love is over. Now the only question will be whether you can give this gift of love to yourself and to another, even as I have given it to you.

All systems, agreements, decisions, and choices that express freedom express God. For God *is* freedom, and freedom is love, expressed.

Remember always that yours is a world of Illusion, that nothing you see is real, and that you may use the Illusion to bring you a grand experience of the Ultimate Reality. Indeed, that is what you have come here to do.

You are living in a dream of your own creation. Let it be the dream of a lifetime, for that is exactly what it is.

Dream of a world in which the God and Goddess in you is never denied, and in which you never again deny the God and the Goddess in another. Let your greeting, both now and forevermore, be *Namasté*.

Dream of a world in which love is the answer to every

question, the response to every situation, the experience in every moment.

Dream of a world in which Life, and that which supports Life, is the highest value, receives the highest honor, and has its highest expression.

Dream of a world in which freedom becomes the highest expression of Life, in which no one who claims to love another seeks to restrict another, and in which all are allowed to express the glory of their being in measure full and true.

Dream of a world in which equal opportunity is granted to all, equal resources are available to all, and equal dignity is accorded to all, so that all may experience equally the unequaled wonder of Life.

Dream of a world in which judgment is never again visited by one upon another, in which conditions are never again laid down before love is offered, and in which fear is never again seen as a means of respect.

Dream of a world in which differences do not produce divisions, individual expression does not produce separation, and the greatness of The Whole is reflected in the greatness of its parts.

Dream of a world in which there is always enough, in which the simple gift of sharing leads to that awareness—and creates it, and in which every action supports it.

Dream of a world in which suffering is never again ignored, in which intolerance is never again expressed, and in which hatred is never again experienced by anyone.

Dream of a world in which ego is relinquished, in which Superiority is abolished, and in which Ignorance is eliminated from everyone's reality, reduced to the Illusion that it is.

Dream of a world in which mistakes lead not to shame, regrets lead not to guilt, and Judgment leads not to Condemnation.

Dream of these things, and more.

Do you choose them?

Then *dream them into being.*

With the might of your dreams, end the nightmare of your reality.

You can choose this.

Or, you can choose the Illusion.

I have said to you before, through the words of poets and leaders and philosophers: There are those who see things as they are and say, "Why?" And there are those who dream of things that never were and say, "Why not?"

What do you say?

21.

Seizing Your Moment of Grace

Now is the time of your deciding. Now is the hour of choice. You have come—as has your species—to a crossroads.

You will select, in the days and weeks, months and years immediately ahead, how you want life to be on your planet—or if you want life to be on your planet at all.

You will choose either to continue living the Illusion that you have created as if it were real. Or you will choose instead to step away from the Illusion, to see it *as* an Illusion, and to *use* the Illusion in order to experience heaven on earth, and the Ultimate Reality of Who You Really Are.

This is My message to the world:

You *can* create a new kind of civilization. You *can* seek a newer world. The option is yours. The moment is at hand. This is your moment of grace.

Use this moment.

Seize the day.

Begin as you awaken, by seeing yourself as Who You

Really Are, by praising all that you have ever been, and all that you have become. And begin by choosing, in this moment of grace, to become more than you have ever been or ever dreamed of being; to reach beyond your own reach; to remember that nothing is beyond reach.

See yourself as the light that will truly light the world. Declare yourself to be so. Announce it to your heart, and then, *through* your heart, to everyone. Let your actions be your announcement. Fill your world with love.

Know that you are the savior for whom all have waited, come to save everyone whose life you touch from any thought they may ever have that would deny the wonder of who they are, and the glory of their eternal communion with God.

Know that you have come to the room to heal the room. You have come to the space to heal the space. There is no other reason for you to be here.

You are on a journey to mastery, and now it is time to get on with it. Embrace the holy moment. This is My message, and there is more.

Be in the world, do not ignore it. Spirituality does not have to mean finding a cave and hiding out forever. Be in your world but not of it. Live *with* the Illusion, not *within* it. Yet do not abandon it, do not retreat from the world. That is not the way to create a better world, and it is not the way to experience the grandest part of you.

Remember that the world was created *for* you so that you might have a context within which to experience yourself as Who You Really Are.

Now is the time to do that. The world you have created may soon be *uncreated* by the lot of you if you ignore that world much longer, allowing it to go its way while you go yours, involved only in your own day-to-day experiences, and playing little part in seeking to co-create the larger experiences around you.

Look at the world around you. Feel your passion. Let it tell you what part of the world around you that you wish to re-create anew. Then use the tools you have been given to begin that re-creation. Use the tools of your own society: the tools of religion, education, politics, economics, and spirituality. You can make *statements* with these tools, statements of Who You Are.

Do not imagine that spirituality and politics do not mix. Politics *is* spirituality, *demonstrated.*

Do not imagine that economics has nothing to do with spirituality. Your economy reveals your spirituality.

Do not think that education and spirituality can, or should, be separate. For what you teach is who you are—and if that is not spirituality, then what is?

And do not imagine that religion and spirituality are not one and the same. Spirituality is that which builds a bridge between the body, the mind, and the soul. All true religions build a bridge, not a wall.

So be the builder of bridges. Close the gaps that have formed between religions, between cultures, between races, and between nations. Join together what has been put asunder.

Honor your home in the Universe, and be its good steward. Protect your environment and save it. Renew your resources and share them.

Give glory to your God by giving glory to each other. See

God in everyone and help everyone see God in themselves. End your divisions and your rivalries, your competitions and your battles, your wars and all your killing forever. End it. *Put an end to it.* All civilized societies finally do.

This is My message to you, and more.

If you truly desire to experience the world of your highest imagining, then you must love unconditionally, share freely, communicate openly, and create cooperatively. There can be no hidden agendas, no limitations on love, no withholding of anything.

You must decide that you truly are all One, that what is good for another is good for you, that what is bad for another is bad for you, that what you do for another you do for yourself, and that what you do not do for another you do not do for yourself.

Is it possible for you to act like this? Are human beings capable of such splendor?

Yes. I tell you yes, and yes, and a thousand times, yes!

And do not worry that then there will not be enough of "what you are not" left to create a contextual field within which to experience Who You Really Are. The whole Universe is your contextual field! All of your memory, as well.

The elders and the wise among you often exhort you to erect monuments, to create special days and solemn rituals to commemorate your past—your wars, your holocausts, and all your moments of dis-grace. Why commemorate these? you may ask. Why keep bringing up the past? And those elders will say, "Lest we forget."

Their advice is more sound than you know, for in creating a contextual field in memory, you make it unnecessary to do so in the present moment. You truly can say "Never again," and mean it. And in declaring this, you *use* your moments of dis-grace to create moments of grace.

Can your species make such a declaration? Can the human race remember itself as it was when it reflected, in every thought, word, and deed, the image and likeness of God? Are you capable of such splendor?

Yes. I tell you yes, and yes, and a thousand times, yes!

This is how you were meant to be, this is how life was designed to be, before you lost yourself in the Illusions.

It is not too late. No, not nearly too late. You of such glory and wonder, you can do it, you can *be* it. You can *be love.*

Know that through all, I am with you. This is the end of the present communication, but it can never be the end of our collaboration, our co-creation, or our communion. You will always have a conversation with God, you will always enjoy a friendship with God, and you will always be in communion with God.

I will be with you always, even unto the end of time. I can never not be with you, for I *am* you, and you are Me. That is the truth, and all else is an Illusion.

So journey on, My friend, journey on. The world waits to hear *your* message for its salvation.

That message is your life, lived.

You are the prophet whose time has come. For what you demonstrate is true about your life today is an absolute prediction of what will be true about your life tomorrow. This makes you a prophet, indeed.

Your world will change because you are choosing to

change it. Your work is healing more than you know, and your reach extends beyond tomorrow.

All of this is true because you choose to allow the wonder of your communion with Me to be demonstrated in, as, and through you. Choose this often and bring peace to My world.

Become an instrument of My peace.

Where there is hatred, sow love;
Where there is injury, pardon;
Where there is doubt, faith;
Where there is despair, hope;
Where there is darkness, light;
Where there is sadness, joy.
Seek not so much to be consoled, as to console;
to be understood, as to understand;
to be loved, as to love.

For love is Who You Are, and who you have always been. It is all there ever was, is now, and ever shall be.

You have searched for a truth by which to live your life, and I give it to you here, again.

Be love, My Beloved.

Be love, and your long journey to mastery will be over, even as your new journey to bring others to mastery has just begun. For love is all that you are, all that I am, and all that We were ever meant to be.

So be it.

In Closing . . .

This extraordinary communication, which I believe to have been divinely inspired, has addressed many of the final questions I have had about God and about life. Added to the previous *With God* books, it produces a startlingly clear and amazingly consistent cosmology.

To me the most significant "revelation" is that I do not need these five books at all—or anything else, for that matter. The entire cosmology is an Illusion, and the First Illusion is the Illusion of Need.

That is an amazing awareness. It puts into clear and concise terms the definition of Who I Really Am.

I am:

That Which Is Without Need.

Or, simply, *That Which Is.*

Or, more simply, *That.*

This becomes the ultimate statement of Being.

I Am That.

Interestingly, this has been the utterance of all true Masters. I have just never understood it.

Now I do.

All you have to do when things become unclear, when life becomes confusing, is face whatever you are looking at and say, "I am That."

All confusion washes away. All anger and resentment disappears. All dysfunction and discontinuity vanishes. All that is left is you and love, and they are one and the same.

Solutions present themselves automatically in such a state of total awareness. Indeed, the grandest solution is the awareness that a problem does not even exist.

Nothing is problematical in the eyes of God.

It is through the eyes of God that you look. You simply do not know this. Until you do. When you do, then you sing out: *Once I was blind, but now I see.*

And this truly is an amazing grace. It is one of your moments of grace—moments of awareness of the Divine—which may come upon you at any time.

I believe that these moments are all part of a process. It is a process that I have come to call remembering. (Others have called it evolution.) It is a process that we are all undergoing.

How does it work?

First, we become aware of that which is Divine around us. Then we become aware of that which is Divine within us. Finally, we become aware that all is Divine, and that there is *nothing else.*

This is the moment of our awakening.

And, once we are awakened, we will want to awaken others. It is only natural. It is what comes next. It is what allows us to function, it is what allows us to experience Who We Really Are.

We will seek opportunities in the world to do this. Some of us will create them.

If we join together in those creations, I believe the creations to have much more power. This is what is meant by *Wherever two or more are gathered in My Name . . .*

I am reminded of the words in a wonderful Christian hymn: *We gather together to ask the Lord's blessing . . .*

One way to do this—and there are many ways, indeed— would be to join with others who have been deeply touched by the message in *Communion with God, Friendship with God,* and the *Conversations with God* trilogy, and who wish that the CWG material could be experienced by everyone.

This message has changed the lives of millions of people, and it has the power to change the world.

We have the power to change the world.

To date, *Conversations with God* has been translated into twenty-seven languages. Its companion books, too, have found their way into homes around the globe. This has produced an enormous upswelling of energy. People everywhere are asking, *How can I make this soul-liberating wisdom a part of my daily life? How can I share it with others?*

When *Conversations with God* was first published in 1995, my wife, Nancy, and I were opening letters and responding to them at our kitchen table. Now those letters are pouring in at the rate of over three hundred a week—with some weeks bringing as many as six hundred! Add to that an equal number of phone calls and e-mails and you can imagine how the time has long since passed when we could keep up with it all.

This incoming energy includes everything from calls for clarification of some of the more challenging material and urgent questions about how it may be applied in day-to-day life, to requests for more educational books, tapes, or programs, to striking and exciting business proposals from people everywhere who have ideas on how to move the message of CWG forward.

Nancy and I have created two organizations—a non-profit foundation, ReCreation, and a profit-making organization, Greatest Visions—in an effort to respond.

The non-profit foundation allows us to do extraordinary work in the world, sharing and applying the message of the *With God* books in many different ways. The profit-making company gives us maximum flexibility in producing the funds that are needed to do that work. After-tax profits from Greatest Visions are donated to ReCreation and other non-profit organizations whose mission is in deep harmony with CWG.

The work undertaken by both organizations has grown to the point where we now receive help from people everywhere who choose to join us in this work, *because they see it as their own.*

Our stated mission is "to give people back to themselves." That is, to return them to the highest expression and the grandest experience and the greatest awareness of what it means to be fully human.

Not many people experience this. Too many humans, still, are living lives of quiet desperation. We can end the desperation. We have never lacked good ideas on how to do that. We have merely lacked the will.

Yet now, more and more, we are gathering the will. More and more, we are seeing what needs to be seen, saying what needs to be said, summoning what needs to be summoned—whatever wisdom, whatever courage, whatever determination—to help people everywhere live the lives they were destined to live, to end our collective nightmare, and to make real our most glorious dream.

More and more we are looking at our world and deciding to re-create ourselves anew in the grandest version of the greatest vision ever we held about Who We Are.

It is with this process of re-creation that both of our organizations are deeply involved. And it is in that process that we invite all people who have been touched by CWG to participate.

There are many levels at which one may "stay connected" with this energy, or become involved in this work.

The newsletter *Conversations* is one way to do so. It may be obtained by sending $35 for 12 issues ($45 outside the U.S.) to "Newsletter," at the ReCreation Foundation address on page 220. *Conversations* contains news of upcoming programs, retreats, seminars, lectures, and other activities, as well as practical, down-to-earth advice on how you can manifest your own greatest vision in your life right now, and my answers to questions from readers around the world.

It also contains a Resource Directory of people, products, programs, and services available nationwide to assist you in your journey to greater spiritual experience and a deeper connection with God. Finally, it contains a special section on Right Livelihood, offering guidance on how to make the message of the *With God* books functional in the marketplace.

Our Empowerment Week program is a very special event offering guidance on deeper understanding of the *With God* material, and practical assistance and advice to those who wish to play
an active role in taking its message into their community, and the
world at large, either as study group facilitators, class instructors,
or retreat and workshop presenters. Empowerment Week provides useful tools with which to share effectively what has touched
your own soul so deeply.

Likewise, our Recreating Yourself five-day Intensive Retreats
offer an extraordinary opportunity to apply the wisdom of CWG
in a functional way in your day-to-day experience—and to re-
create yourself anew.

These and other programs have made our work very exciting,
as has your response to the opportunities they present. We believe
that together we will make a difference.

CWG In Action, for instance, offers you an opportunity to
join hands with others in a membership organization through
which you can help support some extraordinary outreach endeavors, such as . . .

The international forum on using spirituality to end conflict,
in Seoul, South Korea, in June 2001—the work of the New Millennium Peace Foundation, to which *CWG In Action* members
helped give birth.

The Heartlight School Program, a daring new kind of school
with an exciting and innovative curriculum based on the principles of CWG, a pilot project of which is being established in Ashland, Oregon, by the Foundation.

The Wisdom Circle, through which hundreds of people
around the world offer insight on how the CWG material may be

applied to everyday life to people sending us letters, urgently asking for such advice.

Home, Street Home, a program to help those for whom "home, sweet home" is a sidewalk, or a park, or a spot under a bridge. It offers immediate filling of in-the-moment needs, in order to assist people in eventually meeting their own needs—and ultimately seeing, as we all are learning, that Need itself is an Illusion.

CWG In Action membership may be requested with a contribution of $125, which helps—in very direct ways such as described above—to put CWG into action. By joining _CWG In Action_ you send a message of support for what we are doing, and of your decision to add your energies to ours. Members receive a special report, the _Quarterly Update,_ outlining where their money is going and how they are helping to change the world, as well as a handsome certificate from the Foundation in appreciation of the important role they are playing in shifting the paradigm of our collective experience on this planet.

Some of you have indicated an interest not only in helping us spread the message which has touched your life in such a positive way, but in _spreading it with us._

People from all over the world have written to us, asking how they may do this, and whether it is okay.

The answer is, yes, of course. If you feel strongly enough about this material that you wish to share it with others, by all means do so. You need no permission from me. Most of the more than 250 Study Groups around the world (that we know of!) were begun without our even being aware of them. We did not instigate them, or sponsor them in any way.

If you would like our assistance and support as you undertake these wonderful endeavors, contact the Foundation about our Empowered Partners Program. There is no cost involved. The program offers suggestions and guidance, as well as networking opportunities, to those seeking to empower themselves in bringing the CWG message into the world.

For more information about *CWG In Action,* the Empowered Partners Program, our five-day Recreating Yourself retreats, Empowerment Week, or any other aspect of our work, please feel free to get in touch with us at:

The ReCreation Foundation
PMB 1150
1257 Siskiyou Blvd.
Ashland, Oregon 97520
On the Internet at *www.conversationswithgod.org*
Telephone: 541-482-8806
E-mail: *recreating@cwg.cc*

If you would like to propose a product or service connected to the *With God* books that you believe could serve the dual purpose of producing additional income to fuel the CWG vision around the world while creating right livelihood for yourself and others, please contact us at:

Greatest Visions, Inc.
PMB 502
2305-C Ashland Street
Ashland, Oregon 97520
On the Internet at *www.conversationswithgod.org*

Telephone: 541-482-5706
E-mail: mail@greatestvisions.com

God bless you all, and thank you for being with me here, and through the process that has produced the *with God* series. This has been an extraordinary experience, and if it has affected your life to even a fraction of the degree that it has affected mine, I know that we have all been changed in wonderful ways.

Now, shall we change our world?

—NDW

Index